full preparation:
the pfizer guide to
careers in pharmacy

D0833441

A MUST-HAVE GUIDE THAT
PROFILES THE LIFE AND WORK
OF PHARMACISTS IN THE FIELD

Book Editor:
Salvatore J. Giorgianni, PharmD
Director/Team Leader, External Relations
Pfizer Pharmaceuticals Group, Pfizer Inc.

The Pfizer Career Guide Series Editor:
Salvatore J. Giorgianni, PharmD
Director/Team Leader, External Relations
Pfizer Pharmaceuticals Group, Pfizer Inc.

Full Preparation: The Pfizer Guide to Careers in Pharmacy
Assistant Editor: Marlene Lipson

Other Pfizer Career Guide Publications:
Opportunities to Care:
The Pfizer Guide to Careers in Nursing

Embracing Your Practice:
The Pfizer Guide to Careers for Physicians

Advancing Healthy Populations:
The Pfizer Guide to Careers in Public Health

ISBN 0-9602652-1-X

Printed in the United States of America

table of contents

table of contents

acknowledgements

Special appreciation goes to all of the many pharmacists who were willing to put time aside to talk about their daily experiences in practice and the time and skill required to get them where they are today. Through their everyday work and accomplishment, they are just some of the many pharmacists currently paving the way for all those entering the profession.

Daniel Albrant, PharmD

Sara Grimsley Augustin, PharmD, BCPP

Amy Barron, RPh

Jeffrey Binkley, PharmD, BCNSP

J. Chris Bradberry, PharmD

James R. Bresette, PharmD

Bill K. Brewster

Thomas R. Caraccio, PharmD

Carmen Catizone, MS, RPh

Laura Cranston, RPh

John P. Curran, PhD

Diane Darvey, PharmD, JD

Michelle Diamond-Sirota, RPh

Andrew Donnelly, PharmD, MBA

Brian L. Erstad, PharmD

Kate Farthing, PharmD

Salvatore J. Giorgianni, PharmD

William C. Gong, PharmD, FASHP, FCSHP

Judith B. Sommers Hanson, PharmD

Holly Whitcomb Henry RPh, BCPS

Renee Jarnigan, RPh

Vivian Bradley Johnson, PharmD, MBA, FASHP

Paul Jungnickel, PhD, RPh

Commander Brian Kerr, RPh, MS, MBA

Elizabeth K. Keyes, RPh

Alicia Kniska, BS, PharmD, BCOP

Robert Kuhn, PharmD

Henri R. Manasse, Jr., PhD, ScD, RPh

Michael Manolakis, PharmD, PhD

Pat McGowen, BS, RPh, CDE

Mary Meyer, PharmD

Don Michalski, RPh, MS

Walter Miller, PharmD, BCNP

Tricia New, PharmD, FCSHP

Jack Nicolais, RPh, MS

Robert C. Owens Jr., PharmD

Richard Penna, PharmD

Denise H. Rhoney, PharmD

Edward D. Rickert RPh, JD

Edith A. Rosato, RPh

Elisabeth J. Ross, MA

Steven Vollmer, RPh

Alice Angelica Wen, PharmD

Susan C. Winckler, RPh, JD

Finally, and most important, the expertise, guidance and everyday support from J. Lyle Bootman, PhD, Dean, College of Pharmacy, Professor of Pharmacy, Medicine and Public Health, Arizona Health Sciences Center, University of Arizona was instrumental in the development of this book. Thank you.

a letter from pfizer

Dear Pharmacy Student:

Congratulations on your choice of profession. A vast and rewarding array of opportunities within the ever-evolving field of pharmacy awaits you.

As you read through the pages of this guide, you will become familiar with a host of pharmacists who share their stories of challenges, success and professional fulfillment in their everyday practice experience. You'll gain information on the multitude of organizations and associations that support the profession, whether to advocate, educate or simply provide a forum for networking. When you are finished, hopefully you will be armed with the information you need to evaluate the many paths before you and empowered to shape your future. We encourage you to use the resources provided in this guide to obtain additional information in any of the areas that might have peaked your interest.

As a leading global research-based healthcare company, Pfizer is pleased to be a resource to which you can turn for information. Tomorrow's pharmacist faces many more choices than ever before, and the careers summarized in this book simply illustrate the promise before you. We at Pfizer will be with you every step of the way in your professional career. We wish you much success on the road ahead.

Sincerely,

Salvatore J. Giorgianni, PharmD

By Salvatore J. Giorgianni, PharmD
Director – External Relations, Pfizer Pharmaceutical Group and Pfizer Career Guide Series Editor

the future of pharmacy

By J. Lyle
Bootman PhD,
Dean, College
of Pharmacy,
Professor of
Pharmacy,
Medicine and
Public Health,
Arizona Health
Sciences Center,
University of
Arizona

We are living in the most exciting period in the history of pharmaceuticals, as new options lead to new opportunities for those of us in the field and those about to join us. Pharmacists are at a zenith in our ability to manage, cure and prevent disease. Demographics in this country practically

ensure a bright future for those entering the profession. We're witnessing a double dynamic in our population: growth in the number of births and an extended lifespan for men and women.

The record number of baby-boomers graduating into Social Security pensioners has set the stage for an increased use of drugs. When Medicare kicks in for the largest group of elderly ever seen, there will be a pronounced increase in pharmaceutical usage. It is estimated that the number of Americans over 65, now 38 million, will mushroom to 80 million in the next decade. Add to the mix the continuing discovery of new drugs and it's easy to understand why, over the next few years, the number of prescriptions dispensed is expected to more than double.

Somewhat new on the horizon is the idea that pharmacists can operate, by choice, in both a macro- and microcosm. Pharmacists are responsible not only for the management of medications in a macroscopic sense, that is, globally, but in a microscopic sense as well. Interacting one-on-one with their patients will minimize risks of drug-related problems and maximize therapeutic benefits. We teach patients how to read labels, store their medicines, and safely dispose of expired, unused drugs. We also serve to recognize and prevent adverse medication reactions.

Not long ago, people filled prescriptions content to comply with their physician's instructions. No one ever questioned what they were taking. In fact, few people outside the healthcare field really knew much about which new drugs were available, or which worked best and why. Today, one need only turn on the television or pick up a magazine to learn about the explosion of new prescription drugs. People absorbing this information are becoming more educated and informed consumers. It also appears that an increasing number of consumers are intent on participating in their own healthcare, and when they do, they tend to turn to their neighborhood pharmacist for assistance.

Recent studies show consumers interact with their pharmacist 12 to 15 times a year compared to three or four times a year with their physicians. Often when minor symptoms erupt, the first place a patient heads is to the pharmacy, essentially throwing the pharmacist into the triage role.

As the demand for pharmacists grows, their need for in-depth knowledge of emerging medications grows. The first complete map of the human genome, released in the year 2000, dramatically increased the number of potential targets for therapeutic drugs. This brilliant development led to unlimited opportunities for drug discovery. Research and design is an exciting sub-specialty for pharmacists as hundreds of new medications are expected to arrive on the market each year. Currently, 316 drugs are in clinical trials for cancer alone, with thousands more expected to be in the pipeline.

And thanks to pharmacogenomics — the study of how genetic variations account for differences in the way individuals respond to different drugs — therapies are likely to be more effective. In the past, people suffering from diseases had few options to cure or soothe their health problems. Soon, many patients will see a bright light on the horizon.

While pharmacy researchers uncover these drugs, it is the practicing pharmacist who will communicate with patients about proper usage. As it now stands, almost all drugs come with a package insert of information regarding use, appropriate dosages, side effects and which drug combinations to avoid. People have come to expect this information and turn to their pharmacist with any questions before taking medication.

As proof of the public's confidence in their pharmacists, the profession is continually ranked by the Gallup Poll as the most trustworthy profession. Holding such a respected place in the healthcare system is a point of pride among pharmacists, earned through their dedication to ending pain and suffering. Pharmacists serve in all areas of healthcare from community pharmacies to cutting-edge research, applying their unique knowledge of the power and potential of medications.

Dr. Bootman is Dean of the University of Arizona College of Pharmacy. He is a Professor of Pharmacy, Medicine and Public Health. He is the Founding and Executive Director of the University of Arizona Center for Health Outcomes and PharmacoEconomic (HOPE) Research, one of the first such centers developed in the world. He is a former President of the American Pharmaceutical Association and has been named one of America's most influential pharmacists by The American Druggist *magazine. Dr. Bootman received his pharmacy education at The University of Arizona and his doctorate at The University of Minnesota. Additionally, he completed a clinical pharmacy residency at the world-renowned National Institutes of Health. Dr. Bootman has authored over 200 research articles and monographs and has been an invited speaker at more than 350 professional healthcare meetings and symposia. He has received numerous outstanding scientific achievement awards, most notably from the American Association of Pharmaceutical Scientists and the American Pharmaceutical Association. He was the recipient of the George Archambault Award, the highest honor given by the American Society of Consultant Pharmacists and has been awarded the Latiolais Honor Medal, the highest honor in managed healthcare. He has published several books, including the groundbreaking* Principles of Pharmacoeconomics, *which is used in more than 35 countries and has been translated into six languages. His research regarding the outcomes of drug-related morbidity and mortality receives worldwide attention by the professional and public media. He serves as an advisor to leading pharmaceutical companies, universities and healthcare organizations throughout the world. Dr. Bootman is one of only a handful of pharmacists in the prestigious Institute of Medicine of the National Academy of Sciences.*

building your CV

To the future pharmacist:
You will soon graduate from Pharmacy school. The one step left between you and the job of your dreams is *getting that job*. And make no mistake. For the most part, entry through the gateway to that position rests on one small document: your resume. The main objective of this two page "outline of your life" is to present you in the best possible light, and to assure, at the very least, that all-important interview. Listed below are ten basic steps involved in crafting a job-winning resume:

By Brian L. Erstad, PharmD, Associate Professor, Department of Pharmacy Practice & Science, College of Pharmacy, University of Arizona

1. **Your resume should accurately reflect who you are, but it should do so in a certain format and cover specific areas.**
   Seek out a faculty advisor and ask him or her if your pharmacy school has a certain recommended model for you to follow. Those guidelines should be an excellent framework to adopt for your resume. Searching the Internet for recommended formats will also yield excellent templates you can use.

2. **It is very important to adhere to resume standards.**
   The document should be clear, succinct and mistake-free. It is always good to have a few people review it before it is distributed. After you've seen it time and again, the tendency is to gloss over typos or grammatical errors that a fresh pair of eyes might catch. It may seem insignificant, but using white or off-white paper for your resume is essential. Also, laser-generated or commercial printing gives any document a professional look.

3. **What you choose to include — the "meat" of your resume is, of course, essential.**
   I strongly believe that honesty is the best policy. (A recent survey notes that 14 percent of professionals fabricate some parts of their resumes.) Claiming, for example, that you did research or participated in projects that, in fact, you have not, is both unethical and unwise. Exaggerating or claiming things that you think a prospective employer may want to hear can land you in a position that you may not be equipped to handle.

4. **There are clearly tactics that you can and should use to illustrate who you are and what you have accomplished while in pharmacy school.** All pharmacy students will have done some amount of clinical activity. Try to point out unique activities that other candidates may not have done. Perhaps there's a research experience you've had. Or perhaps you've been involved in obtaining some type of grant. Maybe you've published something in a peer review journal. There is nothing wrong with describing these or any awards you have received. Also, it's helpful when describing yourself to weave in words like "quality" or "resourceful."

5. **Get involved early on with student pharmaceutical associations.** Beyond the immediate collegiality, there's the long-term benefit: this should be a real asset and a critical distinguishing aspect. Being an officer in a student group demonstrates leadership ability and commitment to your profession.

6. **Place the most important information about yourself first, but make sure your honors and awards are near the top of the list as well.** Describe anything that will allow the reader to see your personal side because it can make you stand out in the crowd.

7. **If you're applying for a specialty field and you have had experience in that field, you can certainly bold any items related to it.**

8. **Your cover letter should be short and to the point.** It should emphasize those unique features that make you a superior candidate, and should briefly tell why you want this position.

9. **The length of your resume varies depending on an individual's experiences, but for most students it should be a page or two.** Keep the "fluff" to a minimum, or leave it out. Readers prefer to read only the succinct points.

10. **While most people indicate that references are available upon request, list the names along with the addresses and phone numbers of people you think will be helpful if they have agreed to vouch for you.**

Fortunately, with today's shortage of pharmacists, the job climate is in your favor. I wish you the best of luck.

Brian L. Erstad, PharmD is an Associate Professor and Assistant Department Head at the Department of Pharmacy Practice & Science, College of Pharmacy, University of Arizona. His practice site is the University Medical Center in Tucson where he serves as a clinical pharmacist for surgery. Born in South Dakota, Dr. Erstad received a Bachelor of Science in Pharmacy degree from South Dakota State University in 1976 and a Doctor of Pharmacy degree from The University of Arizona in 1987. He worked as a staff pharmacist at St. Joseph's Hospital in Tucson and at Rapid City Regional Hospital in Rapid City, South Dakota. Dr. Erstad has been largely involved with critical care medicine with an emphasis on plasma expanders such as albumin, perioperative pain control, perioperative antimicrobial therapy, and sedation. His CV lists dozens of honors and awards.

words of wisdom

By Richard
Penna,
PharmD,
Executive Vice
President,
American
Association of
Colleges of
Pharmacy

Pharmacy is a very old profession and has changed profoundly over the years. I'm nearing retirement and have had the opportunity to see our profession change, expand and mature over 40 years. It is a dynamic, growing, and increasingly diverse profession, one which creates an excitement because there are so many opportunities for service. The secret in the future will be to identify and take advantage of these opportunities.

I am a hiker, and when I'm off a trail, sometimes I find myself on unfamiliar terrain. When that happens, I keep my bearings by establishing landmarks, focusing on things that don't change, like the river below me or a distant mountain. These serve as my personal points of reference, keeping me connected to my bearings so that I can enjoy the changing scenery. You should identify and use landmarks in your future profession also. One of the landmarks you can orient your compasses on is the fact that drug use isn't going to change. Pharmacotherapy is currently the most frequently used form of medical intervention in this country and will, it appears, remain so. In fact, it is expected that the number of drug products available to treat people will continue to grow exponentially as the population ages.

Another landmark is that people will demand personal attention. As drugs continue to increase in potency, risk, and cost, patients are going to need more personal care. Over the past 25 years, pharmacy has introduced the concept of individual involvement with the patient (clinical pharmacy). More recently, we introduced the concept of pharmaceutical care, which posits that pharmacists have a personal responsibility for their patients. Like our sister profession, nursing, which has long been held in high regard, pharmacy also has adopted a personal, caring role. Combine the pharmacist's knowledge of drugs with his or her concern for the welfare of the consumer and you have the makings of a benevolent profession.

Pharmacists can't stop moving. It's the natural order of what we do. That's because new drugs are constantly coming out and we must continually educate ourselves about them to stay abreast of the latest and best treatments. If we fall behind, we'll fail in our commitment to our patients. As a pharmacist, you must periodically re-invest in your education — returning for refresher courses every so often to learn about the latest developments in the field.

What sets us apart from physicians and nurses is our expansive knowledge of the physical and chemical properties of a vast number of drugs (the pharmaceutical sciences). We expect a strong focus on chemistry. It is imperative to know how one slight change in a molecule can make all the difference in the world in some patients.

The demand for pharmacists will remain strong throughout your careers. And should you want it, there will be opportunities for independent practice that will grow over time. The pharmacist in the white coat standing behind the counter dispensing medication has already expanded to new opportunities. Today some pharmacists maintain private offices and see patients to manage complicated drug therapies. As the population ages and drug use becomes more necessary and complicated, these will continue to expand. So should your interest in exploring them.

Richard P. Penna, PharmD, is Executive Vice President of the American Association of Colleges of Pharmacy, the organization representing the interests of pharmaceutical education and educators. Dr. Penna received his Doctor of Pharmacy degree from the University of California School of Pharmacy, San Francisco in 1959. He practiced community pharmacy for eight years and taught pharmacy practice at his alma mater for five years. Dr. Penna joined the staff of the American Pharmaceutical Association (APhA) in 1966. While at APhA, he directed projects which included revising and publishing three editions of the APhA Handbook of Nonprescription Drugs. In addition, he served as APhA Vice President for Professional Affairs. Dr. Penna joined the staff of the American Association of Colleges of Pharmacy in January 1985 as Associate Executive Director. He was appointed Executive Vice President in July 1995.

By Holly
Whitcomb
Henry, RPh,
BCPS, President,
Medicine
Ladies, Inc.,
Regional
Director,
Carepoint
Pharmaceutical
Care
Consultants,
Clinical
Associate
Professor,
University of
Washington
School of
Pharmacy

professional overview

the role of the pharmacist as part of the healthcare team

In a sense, pharmacy practice is a "back-to-the-future" story. In the early days of American pharmacy, pharmacists served in the role of community caregivers, diagnosing ailments and then managing them by compounding individual remedies. With the advent of commercialized drug production, increased regulation and legislative action, evolved standards of practice in many ways impeded patient interactions rather than encouraging them. Pharmacists from the 1940s to the 1960s did not routinely counsel patients and did not even customarily put the name of the dispensed drug on the drug label. That protocol was reversed in the late 1970s. Washington became the first state to require pharmacists to counsel patients about new prescriptions and to keep a running profile of each customer's medications. By the 1980s, pharmacists were once again playing a more integral role in direct patient care.

Today, the pharmacist plays an essential role as part of the healthcare team. Our professional responsibilities cover five essential areas:

1. **Drug delivery and medication safety.**

   Under our model of care, physicians generally head the healthcare team, while the pharmacist enters the patient care continuum after the prescription has been written. Delivering the right drug, identifying the correct dosage and times it is to be taken, labeling it clearly, and listing potential side effects are all part of the pharmacist's well-known responsibilities. But today's drugs are considerably more complex than they once were — and with genomes, biotechs and genetic compounding, drug therapy stands to grow even more individualized over the next ten years. The pharmacist's role is concurrently expanding.

   Maximizing the safety of medications is an increasingly critical responsibility of our practice. Each new prescription demands that the pharmacist review it in conjunction with other information we have about the patient. The average person sees 2.3 prescribers every year and uses 1.2 pharmacies, studies report. Fortunately, people are pretty loyal to their pharmacies. That makes it possible for us to cross-check their medications and catch drug interactions from different prescribers. It is a critical role that the pharmacist is in the best position to perform.

2. Patient education and advocacy.

The rule of mandatory counseling was initiated by the federal government on all prescriptions for which it paid. Today, offers to counsel are obligatory on all new prescriptions in every state. It is the pharmacist's task to be sure the patient knows the name of the drug, what it is for, how and when it is to be taken, how to minimize possible interactions with other drugs (prescription or OTC) and foods, and optimal storage. Asking open-ended questions like "What has the doctor told you about this medication?" helps. But even where the prescriber or nurse has explained, the patient may not have heard or perhaps didn't understand, making the pharmacist a critical checkpoint.

3. Monitoring drug therapy.

Pharmacists play a key role in helping patients maximize their pharmaceutical care. For example, it is estimated that up to fifty percent of all patients on medication for hypertension do not have their pressure under control because they lack regular follow-up. Pharmacists are ideally suited to track individuals on these medications and help them obtain proper follow-up. Americans are typically in their local pharmacy at least once or twice a month. Many come in weekly. It is apparent how convenient it is to have blood pressure machines set up, so patients can check their numbers and have the pharmacist explain what those numbers mean. Since most insurance companies mandate refills every 30 days, this is a particularly useful service that provides a perfect opportunity to involve patients in their own care.

As part of the healthcare team, the pharmacist can act as a support system in disease management programs. This is a more progressive role than when I was licensed to practice 23 years ago. Some interesting new models for care are evolving. One such model has pharmacists selecting from agreed-upon therapeutic options and then working directly with the patient to maximize outcomes. Physicians might prescribe not a specific product, but an outcome — say, the desire to lower blood pressure to a specific level with pharmaceuticals. Recognizing our expertise, many forward-thinking physicians are also asking us to recommend specific drugs or work out schedules to taper chemical-dependent patients off certain drugs.

Many states are headed in this direction. In 1977, Washington became the first state to legislate collaborative therapy whereby physicians can delegate prescription authority to pharmacists. Another 20 states have followed suit and this topic is on the legislative agenda of many other states as well.

One of the major barriers to our operating as prescribers is that, thus far, we are not paid to do so. A bill in the Senate in the spring of 2001 includes giving pharmacists provider numbers for Medicare recognition. We have already broken the barrier by giving flu shots. Last year our company's pharmacy clinics administered 3,000 of them. That was a first important step in having Medicare recognize us. Providing reimbursement for diabetes, cholesterol and blood pressure management are new goals our profession is currently pursuing.

4. **Teaming with other health care providers.**
    Pharmacists do not work alone. We interact daily with physicians and, more often, with office nurses. We also work with PA's, NP's and other prescribers, including dentists and veterinarians. We regularly collaborate with nursing home staffs, reviewing patient charts every month for drug interactions and adverse side effects. A federal mandate for the past 20 years, the nursing home rule has resulted in fewer medication-related problems and in patients taking fewer drugs. In the teamwork model, pharmacists play a key role.

5. **Research and clinical studies.**

People trust their local pharmacists. Our strong relationships in the community are newly appreciated by medical professionals. So much so that pharmacists now play a participating role in clinical studies. Increasingly, pharmacists are being recruited to do community-based research in the post-marketing surveillance of drugs.

Routine screenings are another way pharmacists can promote wellness. A recent Impact Study from the American Pharmaceutical Association of 400 patients recruited by 30 pharmacies found that quarterly coaching or feedback on how well patients were managing their cholesterol boosted patient compliance with therapy from 37 percent to 94 percent a year after diagnosis.

I am happy I chose to be a pharmacist. My profession gives me the ability to have an impact on people's lives, to make a real and positive difference. Hardly a day goes by that someone doesn't thank me — and that truly feels wonderful.

Holly Whitcomb Henry, RPh, BCPS, a board-certified pharmacotherapy specialist, is president of Medicine Ladies, Inc., a Seattle, Washington-based corporation, owning and operating four local pharmacies that employ 10 pharmacists since 1986. She serves as a Clinical Professor at the University of Washington School of Pharmacy, and is also part of the Clinical Affiliate Faculty for Washington State University College of Pharmacy.

After completing a Bachelor of Pharmacy degree from Washington State University College of Pharmacy in 1978, Ms. Henry worked as a staff pharmacist at Pay 'N' Save Corporation in Seattle, Washington. She then became Executive Assistant Director of the Washington State Pharmacists Association in May 1980. For much of her 5-year tenure, she was also Editor of The Washington Pharmacist.

In July 1991, Ms. Henry completed an American Pharmaceutical Association Apple/SKB Residency in Community Pharmacy Management and, in June 1995, completed a Certificate Program in Geriatric Pharmacy from the University of Washington School of Pharmacy. She is active in pharmacy associations, having served as President of the Washington State Pharmacists Association in 1998–99. She currently serves on the Executive Committee of the National Community Pharmacists Association.

By Carmen A.
Catizone, MS,
RPh, Executive
Director of the
National
Association of
Boards of
Pharmacy
(NABP),
Secretary of the
Association's
Executive
Committee

professional overview
ethics, regulations and standards of pharmacy

Pharmacy is one of the most regulated professions in the country and one of the most ethically challenging. State boards of pharmacy regulate, administer and influence every phase of pharmacy practice, including the requirements and testing to become a licensed pharmacist. Each state board is made up of pharmacists who come from every practice area — hospitals, chains, independent pharmacies — as well as at least one consumer (non-pharmacist) representative. In most states, pharmacy board members are appointed by the governor.

The mission of the state pharmacy boards is to set regulations, standards, and parameters within which pharmacists practice. The boards also monitor compliance with these standards so that pharmacists clearly understand what is expected of them and what support they can expect in return. Three of the more important regulations set by state boards ensure that pharmacists conduct a patient history, check a patient's current medications for any possible drug interactions, and interact with the patient directly. Other key standards of practice focus on the dispensing of drugs: the limits on how various classes of drugs may be sold, how prescriptions are secured, what special forms are required for strict-access drugs, and the confidentiality of patient information. The standards set by the boards are a cooperative effort among pharmacy professionals, the state legislature and consumer groups. Our profession is represented through its associations and through individual pharmacists who belong to these associations.

Protecting the public is the primary goal of pharmacy boards. On a broad scale, this mission requires a pharmacist to attend school for a specific number of years and to pass the state competency examination. Boards also set the parameters for what happens if a law or regulation is violated, what penalties result, and what infractions can cause a pharmacist to lose his or her license. A classic example of the latter is a person engaged in the practice of drug diversion — selling prescription medications for profit or selling narcotics on the street. State pharmacy boards determine what can and cannot be dispensed. They set up "drug schedules" that determine the stringency of requirements for dispensing specific medications. Responding to and investigating patient complaints about the behavior of individual pharmacists is another critical charge of the state boards.

Each state has its own board of pharmacy that regulates pharmacists and pharmaceuticals in that state. Each state board belongs to the National Association of Boards of Pharmacy (NABP). At the NABP, we have no legal authority *per se* but, in our capacity as a national advisory group, we have a significant influence in helping states develop regulations, thereby insuring a standard of consistency across all 50 states. The NABP has issued recommended regulations, for example, that all patients should be counseled and that Internet pharmacies should receive certification. In general, our recommendations are typically accepted and adopted by the state boards. The NABP also develops and administers the national licensing exam for pharmacy students used by all states except California.

As in any profession regulated by strict laws and guidelines, ethical dilemmas inevitably arise that challenge the pharmacist to rely upon his or her own moral compass. For example, in today's ultra-busy and frequently understaffed pharmacies, the issue of patient counseling has become a difficult area for many pharmacists. Because studies have proved that counseling enhances patient compliance and can help the pharmacist to uncover areas of potential concern, state boards have made patient interaction a normal standard of practice. While every pharmacist wants to make decisions in the patient's very best interest, a burdensome real-life workload can make these kinds of meaningful conversations and exchanges of information difficult to accomplish. Time constraints can also discourage pharmacists who are motivated to check back with a prescriber. In our changing healthcare climate, these are complicated questions indeed.

Answers will come, of course. In fact, these are areas where dedicated young pharmacists can have considerable impact. One of the most valuable things a young pharmacist can do is to get involved with his or her own state pharmacy board. By attending meetings, interacting with board members and becoming involved in their state's practice issues, new pharmacists can have significant influence in such areas as working conditions for pharmacists and making practice more clinical and less dispensing. Young board members can help to redefine the practice of pharmacy to be more reflective of current trends and conditions. Having a voice will allow the new generation of professionals to realize some of their own dreams for the direction in which pharmacy is headed.

Carmen A. Catizone, MS, RPh is the Executive Director of the National Association of Boards of Pharmacy (NABP) and Secretary of the Association's Executive Committee. NABP is an international organization whose purpose is to assist the state boards of pharmacy in protecting the public health and welfare, and to serve as an information and disciplinary clearinghouse for the interstate transfer of licensing among the state boards of pharmacy. The organization is also charged with issuing model regulations in order to assist the state boards of pharmacy with the development of uniform practice as well as education and competency standards for the practice of pharmacy.

Mr. Catizone graduated from the University of Illinois at Chicago College of Pharmacy with a Bachelor of Science degree in pharmacy and a Master of Science degree in pharmacy administration. His master's studies focused on healthcare policy/planning and the history of pharmacy. He is an actively practicing pharmacist, past president of the National Pharmacy Manpower Project (1989–96) and the National Conference of Pharmaceutical Organizations (1995), and a reviewer on several advisory boards. Mr. Catizone is the recipient of the Certificate of Appreciation from the District of Columbia (1990), the Food and Drug Administration's Commissioner's Special Citation (1994), the University of Illinois Alumnus of the Year (1997), and American Druggist's Pharmacist of the Year award (1998).

practice areas

chapter one
academic pharmacist

A TRUE TALE

J. Chris Bradberry, PharmD, chairman of Pharmacy Practice and Pharmacoeconomics at the University of Tennessee loves the variety being

an academic pharmacist affords. He also enjoys the autonomy, and the great relationship he has with students, physicians and residents. But the best thing about his job, Dr. Bradberry says, is feeling "as if I'm helping to shape the future of our profession." As an academic pharmacist, Dr. Bradberry has enormous freedom to pursue his interests.

An early fascination led him into the field. When he was eight years old, Dr. Bradberry was captivated by the mysterious vials and chemicals in the old fashioned, family run apothecary in Lafayette, South Louisiana where he grew up. The pharmacist there, sensing his keen attention, often invited him behind the counter to explore her world. "It was like a pilot inviting a would-be young flyer into the cockpit," he says.

Dr. Bradberry's interest in pharmacy grew through school. After a two-year pre-pharmacy program at Loyola University in New Orleans, he earned a baccalaureate degree in pharmacy from the University of Louisiana at Monroe Pharmacy School in 1967. Two years later, after a graduate program at a major teaching center in New Orleans, Dr. Bradberry experienced a bit of what he lightheartedly refers to as "culture shock" when he joined the United States Public Health Service. As a commissioned officer, he spent the next two years as the chief pharmacy officer in a large clinic on a rural Navajo reservation in Arizona, which is part of the Indian Health Service. There, he was one of three pharmacists serving 15,000 people, where most of the conditions were related to infectious disease.

"A pharmacist practicing on a Navajo reservation," Dr. Bradberry says, "definitely faces challenges." In Arizona many in the Navajo community still consulted medicine men and their own health belief system. "It was important for those of us practicing western medicine to blend our cultures and belief systems. We had interpreters and learned a bit of their language but often relied on picture labels to explain to them how they should take medication."

Academic Pharmacist Checkpoint

Do you find joy in teaching and researching?

Are you creative in coming up with productive programs?

Will you be a resourceful team player?

If so, read on

Dr. Bradberry returned to graduate school and was awarded a Doctor of Pharmacy degree from the University of Tennessee in 1972. After a yearlong residency in pharmacy at the University of Texas at Galveston, he was recruited to join the faculty at the University of Nebraska. Although he was there just briefly, the experience convinced him that academia offered an opportunity to be a leader, mentor and educator. "I was delighted to see how much I enjoyed the student contact, and the gratification it brought," he says.

After leaving Nebraska, Dr. Bradberry spent time at the University of Texas, University of Oklahoma and finally transferred to University of Tennessee, where he is now. Dr. Bradberry quips that his resume suggests "I just can't keep a job." Instead, he feels moving around has provided him with a broader view to share with student and other academic pharmacists through his teaching.

Profiling the job

Over 3,000 full-time faculty members work in the nation's 82 colleges of pharmacy. Thousands more are involved in mentoring at various levels from community checkups to research fellows. They are involved with teaching, research, public service and sometimes, patient care. Others work as consultants for local, state, national, and international organizations, teaching and doing research, much of which involves investigational pharmacotherapeutics, and epidemiological studies.

The University of Tennessee College of Pharmacy enrolls 100 students in each class in a four-year program. There are 60 faculty members dispersed among pharmacy science, clinical pharmacy and pharmacy practice. As head of the pharmacy practice unit, Dr. Bradberry focuses mainly on primary and ambulatory care.

"I am trying to be a role model so students take the best things I can offer in terms of professional responsibilities and ethics and apply it to their own careers."

The pharmacy curriculum at the University of Tennessee generally begins with two and a half years in didactic work, which includes lectures and conferences. "We typically work with small groups of students (about 10) in the first year so we can get to know them," Dr. Bradberry says, "and it gives them a perspective of pharmacy from a faculty point of view. We teach a critical thinking course in the

first year in which senior faculty lead discussions that include subjects like ethics, career choices and problem solving issues."

Later, as students get into the second half of their third year, they start a clinical rotation under supervision. Third year also includes a sequence of conferences that simulate the clinic in which faculty serve as mentors to facilitate students' getting ready to see patients.

"There are sequences of drug therapy management courses that the third years take and I generally teach about lipid disorder and treatment, which is my specialty." One month at a time, through the fourth year, students rotate much like they do in the clinical years in medicine. Pharmacy students experience community, hospital, critical, care, and clinic settings.

A day in the life

For three half days a week, Dr. Bradberry teaches students subjects from the standard pharmacy curriculum. In addition, as part of his teaching responsibilities, Dr. Bradberry takes two senior pharmacy students and a resident, to see patients at a public clinic that is part of the University. These ambulatory patients, most of whom are middle aged to elderly, have been referred by physicians for medication management of their conditions, most of which are chronic. Dr. Bradberry shows the students how to streamline their medication and how to make their regimes more user friendly so they will be compliant. This is essentially teaching students to take what he has taught in the classroom and apply it to people who will one day be their patients. While the students listen, he makes recommendations, dosage changes and advises new therapeutic regimens. He tries to instill in his students the same efficiency he was taught years ago and to help them gain confidence dealing with patients and relating to them on an empathetic level.

But teaching students is only part of a week's work. Dr. Bradberry delivers several didactic lectures a year (his specialty is dyslipidemia). He also publishes several research articles each year. The rest of his work-time is consumed by administrative duties at the university. He provides the direction for experiential education at the school, and makes certain it stays top quality — and he regularly works on faculty development issues, academic course work, scheduling and the budget. Periodically, he serves on committees and with state and national pharmaceutical organizations.

"Being an academic pharmacist means there are many opportunities for you to mentor students, but there is also an opportunity to grow yourself through the need to publish, conduct research and the like."

J. Chris Bradberry, PharmD

Dr. Bradberry works out of a "typical" academic office, aided by an administrative assistant, secretaries and a business manager. He also keeps an office at the clinic. His day is packed with academic duties and most evenings he heads for home with a briefcase stuffed with papers and publications to read.

STUDENT POINT OF VIEW

A 60-year-old man with diabetes was having tremendous difficulty controlling his disease. He wasn't complying with his suggested regime because he didn't understand his nutritional needs. The student sat with Dr. Bradberry and watched him talk at length to the man over a period of several appointments. Within a month, the man had learned so much about the importance of taking his medications that his compliance rate improved remarkably and his blood sugar normalized. The student told Dr. Bradberry that the hands-on experience he achieved through rotations helped him narrow down the areas in which he aspired to practice later in his career.

>>> fast facts

What do you need?
- Ability to balance research and teaching responsibilities with patient care
- Ability to serve as a role model for pharmacy students and residents
- Comfort with sophisticated instrumentation, statistical analyses, and other research methods

What's it take?
- Bachelor of Science (BS), Doctor of Pharmacy (PharmD) and/or PhD degree may be required (depending on the position)*
- One-year residency may be required
- Fellowship is preferred

Where will you practice?
- Universities
- Schools of pharmacy
- Local, state, national, and international organizations

* Students graduating after Spring 2004 will be required to have a PharmD degree

chain drug store pharmacist

A TRUE TALE

When Edith Rosato, RPh, was a Temple University undergraduate trying to decide what her major should be, she had a talk with her brother-in-law, a pharmacist working for a chain drug store. "Pharmacy is a science-based profession with patient or customer involvement," he told her. "And I know you like science, chemistry and people." Soon after, Rosato entered into

pharmacy school and graduated in 1982 with a degree in pharmacy. "The funny thing is, I had worked in a community pharmacy in my hometown of Landsdowne, Pennsylvania since I was 16. But until that conversation, I had never thought of pharmacy as a career."

Rosato believes the field's low visibility is still an issue today. "Kids in school who want to go into a health care profession don't think of pharmacy," she says. Rosato is working to change that. In her current position at the National Association of Chain Drug Stores (NACDS), she strives to stimulate career interest in pharmacy and broadcast the many exciting opportunities open to those graduating from pharmacy school.

While she was attending pharmacy school, Rosato continued to work for a local chain drug store, gaining valuable experience. After graduation, she began her career as a "floater" with that chain, going from store to store, covering vacations, sick-time or as an extra staff pharmacist. Within a few months, Rosato was promoted to pharmacy manager — one of her most rewarding job experiences. "Years ago, the pharmacists managed the entire store operation," she says. As both pharmacy and front-store manager, Rosato learned the retail drug store business from the ground up, including budgeting, inventory control, and personnel management.

After six years, Rosato left for another chain drug store that was new to the Philadelphia area. "As a woman, I thought I'd have an excellent career opportunity with this young start-up company," she says. In her first position as pharmacy manager at CVS, Rosato was responsible for managing the pharmacy department operations. Rosato's instincts about broadening her career opportunities paid off. Within a year and a half of moving to CVS,

Chain Drug Store Pharmacist Checkpoint

Does the business side of pharmacy appeal to you?

Do you like management, administrative and personnel issues?

Do you like the idea of trying different aspects of your career?

If so, read on

Rosato was encouraged by her pharmacy district manager and supervisor to interview for a position in the home office in Woonsocket, Rhode Island as a Pharmaceutical Buyer. Rosato says that she was very fortunate to have been chosen for the job and that it really presented a rare opportunity for her to be promoted up through the ranks of the organization. After a year as an assistant learning the ropes, she became a full purchasing buyer. Her responsibilities included purchasing products for the three distribution centers. "I also worked with the DEA, FDA, EPA, OSHA — all those government agencies — to ensure that CVS complied with all regulations," she explains. Pharmacy buying is a specialty most graduating students don't know about, Rosato says. "It is a busy, fast-paced job. I loved it."

From CVS, Rosato went on to a pharmaceutical company to be a national sales account manager. After a year and a half, she was promoted to the business development department where she remained for six years before moving to NACDS as Vice President of Pharmacy Affairs.

Profiling the job

"In chain store pharmacy, the sky's the limit if you're a go-getter. There are endless opportunities — you can create the career you want," Rosato says. "As a pharmacist, you can practically dictate where you want to be — in the store, the field, or the home office."

Store-based Pharmacist

Entry-level for graduating pharmacists is generally in a store. Typically, the next step is a promotion to pharmacy manager. That job entails overseeing the staff pharmacists, technical help and register help. The pharmacy manager is responsible for inventory budgets, payroll and scheduling.

Field-based Pharmacist

After some tenure as a pharmacy store manager, there may be opportunities in the field as pharmacy district managers. At this level, the assigned territory may include 12 to 14 stores. A district manager generally spends two days working out of a regional office and the other three days traveling from store to store. During store visits, the district manager deals with any issues that come up, including questions about inventory, personnel or general workflow. District managers also guide and counsel in-store pharmacists.

Regional managers have broader responsibilities, usually for 25 to 30 stores. While a regional manager would occasionally make visits to stores, he or she would meet with the district managers regularly in the field and at home headquarters every few months. The regional manager is the direct liaison to corporate headquarters, reporting on sales or operations, or both.

Home Office-based Pharmacist

A number of extraordinary opportunities exist within the chain home office. A career along this path most often starts with working in a chain store environment to learn the business. Depending on the level of expertise that the pharmacist has, he or she can explore the following career paths.

Operations

Like every business, the chain store pharmacy's bottom line must be profitable. A pharmacy operations manager directly oversees the financials of each store: personnel, technology and workflow, professional services, and increasing profitability are all components to a smooth-running pharmacy. Pharmacy operators work with all other departments to provide resources to ensure financial success.

Clinical Services

Strengthening the pharmacy's name and image to both the public and physicians is one of the functions of an effective clinical services department. Working hand-in-hand with the operations department, the clinical services manager must develop education and health programs, often working with community groups and other professionals to assist the public in living healthier. Examples of programs include patient outreach, diabetes screenings and consultations, blood pressure clinics, osteoporosis clinics and immunizations.

Human Resources

With today's shortage of pharmacists, recruiting the entire pharmacy staff is crucial to a successful operation. Moreover, it is critical that all store technicians are properly trained so that they can assist the pharmacist and enhance efficiency. In the chain industry, pharmacists work within the human resources department to develop, implement and improve recruiting and training strategies. Human resource pharmacists visit pharmacy schools where they make presentations, hold career fairs, and provide internship, externship and pharmacist job opportunities.

Technology

More and more pharmacists have pursued
career paths in this area, which ensures that
new technology that is designed is implemented with the primary responsibilities
of the pharmacist in mind. Pharmacists
working in the technology department of
the chain industry are involved with all new
developments which enhance workflow and
save the pharmacist time to interact more
with patients. These pharmacists provide
valuable input to the operations department
in procuring new technology which will
provide an adequate return on investment.

Government Relations

Pharmacists who work in government relations enjoy politics and pharmacy
law. Many who work within the home office in this area have also obtained
a law degree. Within the chain industry, these pharmacists are very active
within each state legislature as well as with the federal government. Whether
it is dealing with FDA regulations, new pharmacy state laws, addressing the
pharmacist shortage, or providing input on prescription programs for the
elderly, these pharmacists provide education to the policymakers of the
pharmacy industry.

Pharmacy Purchasing

Most chains employ pharmacists to oversee the procurement of pharmaceuticals within their corporation. Pharmacists who work in the purchasing
arena are the first to hear about new products before their release. They are
responsible for designing strategies to ensure that all stores have access to
new products as soon as they become available. In addition, these pharmacists
review clinical data, company profiles and drug availability to decide on
appropriate generic providers for their company. Pharmacists who work in
the purchasing department play a huge role in inventory management by
purchasing the right drugs at the right price and enhancing overall profitability.

Managed Care

By definition, chains provide healthcare services for large patient populations. Contracting with employer groups and pharmacy benefit management (PBM) companies is over 80 percent of the business and must be profitable. In the managed care system, the chain works closely with major insurance companies with whom they negotiate contracts based on payment for services. In chains with a mail order component, a pharmacist has a direct relationship with that facility, overseeing proper formulary management and therapeutic interventions. Pharmacists who work within the managed care area of a chain closely interact with those in clinical services in developing compliance programs and other professional services which can be marketed to insurance companies.

A day in the life

Earlier in her career, Rosato was a staff pharmacist and she clearly remembers what a pharmacist's typical day is like. "There is a general misconception that the public has about pharmacists, people think all we pharmacists do is count, lick, stick and pour," she laughs. In reality, there's a lot more to the job. "We are highly trained medication experts with many responsibilities." For example, Rosato cites the quality assurance checks that happen behind the scenes to prohibit drug or dosing interactions that many patients don't know about.

Chain pharmacists also spend time on the phone with physicians, checking things that don't look right, double-checking dosing, or recommending other products if the pharmacist thinks there's a better drug option. "Only after all this do we get the product off the shelf, count it and generate the label," says Rosato. "And this is the point when all those insurance

"If I have a three-year-old child who was prescribed an antibiotic and the dosage seems too high, I'm going to check on that. As well as checking dosages, the pharmacist also asks what other drugs the patient is currently taking. That's why it's critical for patients to always use the same pharmacy — that way, one pharmacy has your complete medical and drug record."

questions kick in." For instance, issues that arise include: Patients' claims are denied for any number of reasons, a product isn't on the insurer's formulary, or prior authorization from the insurance carrier is needed for a very expensive product.

All in all, Rosato feels that whether a pharmacist practices in a chain or elsewhere, a need to educate patients does exist. "I feel we as an industry need to help patients to see their pharmacy as a total health care center, not simply a pill dispensary," says Rosato. "Patients should be encouraged to spend more time talking with us. They should tell their pharmacist what other medications they're taking, what vitamins, what minerals, what herbal supplements. This is all vital information. So vital, in fact, that some chains are now setting up pharmacist counseling sessions for patients with chronic diseases to help them manage their health."

>> >> fast facts

What do you need?
- Endurance to work long hours, often standing up
- Ability to handle multiple tasks and heavy workloads
- Ability to endure high levels of stress
- A desire to help people and improve the quality of their lives
- A strong ability to communicate clearly and effectively
- A team approach and a positive attitude

What's it take?
- A current, active license to practice pharmacy
- Bachelor of Science (BS) or Doctor of Pharmacy (PharmD) degree*

Where will you practice?
- Traditional chain drugstores
- Supermarket pharmacies
- Mass merchandiser pharmacies

*Students graduating after Spring 2004 will be required to have a PharmD degree

community pharmacist

A TRUE TALE

Jack Nicolais, RPh, MS, sole owner of Saxon Chemists in White Plains, New York, is a happy man. Every day he wakes up feeling blessed. "I have never missed a payroll or paid our rent late. And recently I've been able to offer my employees a 401K," he says proudly. "I have always made a decent living and despite the fact that I work 70 hours a week, I've always loved

the major aspects of being a local pharmacist — the medical community, the patients, the problem solving and most of all, the fact that I'm the one I rely on."

Just as he enjoys the social contact being a community pharmacist affords, Nicolais also revels in the fact that he is a small business owner. That interest percolated when, as a boy, he often accompanied his mother to a local drug store in Queens, New York, and was completely entranced by the white-coated professionals who clearly knew medicine but also ran the rest of the business. As soon as he was old enough to obtain working papers, Nicolais began clerking in a pharmacy. It gave him the opportunity to experience every aspect of the business. All this fascinated him to the point that he continued working there throughout high school. After that, he attended and graduated from the Albany College of Pharmacy and got his master's degree in pharmacy management from St. John's University in New York City.

His next step was a job. The best ones available were in hospital pharmacies, and he worked his way up to the role of director in two of them. But his love remained the small, independent, neighborhood pharmacy, and so when the opportunity to become a partner at Saxon Chemists arose, he jumped at the opportunity. Eventually, a few years later, when Nicolais's two partners decided that was a good time to retire, Nicolais bought them out and became the sole owner of the business.

Community Pharmacist Checkpoint

Do you feel a personal commitment to making people feel better?

Would you have the patience to help people sift through the hurdles of insurance?

Are you business oriented and able to think in terms of the bottom-line?

If so, read on

Profiling the job

Occupying a downtown storefront on a main street in a mixed neighborhood across from city-owned public housing, Saxon Chemists is visited by between 250 and 300 customers and patients each day. Jack Nicolais knows — or at least recognizes — almost all of them. Not surprising, because many people today tend to see their community pharmacist more than their healthcare providers. In fact, pharmacists are said to receive more than two billion inquiries a year from their patients.

> "Of the many challenges that face today's and tomorrow's community pharmacists, the coming into maturity of the baby-boomer generation is among the most problematic. By the year 2005, it is estimated that four billion prescriptions will be dispensed in the outpatient setting, yet the number of pharmacists is not slated to increase in a comparable proportion."
>
> Laura Cranston, RPh

Nicolais says he advises patients not just about curative treatments, but about preventive medicine as well. On average the pharmacy fills around 300 prescriptions a day, of which three to five are compounded on the premises. The most common drugs he dispenses are for high cholesterol and ulcers. The most unusual? Antibiotics for a pet parakeet. With six of every ten pharmacists in America providing care to patients in a community setting, the business is booming.

On a community level, it is estimated that independent pharmacies dispense 1.1 billion prescriptions annually. In fact, last year the average community pharmacy had $1.97 million in sales, $1.64 million of which was from prescription drugs.

A day in the life

As a community pharmacist, Nicolais keeps long hours. During the week, Saxon opens at 8:00am and closes at 7:00pm. On weekends and holidays it opens an hour later. Nicolais manages the store and fills prescriptions. There are two other pharmacists on staff to help. In addition, there are two pharmacy assistants who, under the direction of one of the pharmacists, measure dosage forms, and label bottles. This enables the pharmacists to get out from behind the counter and talk to customers.

Running one of the nearly 25,000 independent pharmacies in the nation, Nicolais must respond quickly to market conditions and consumer needs. Keeping customers loyal in an open market also presents challenges to a businessperson's innovativeness. He has renovated the store twice, completely changing the product mix and atmosphere of his store. Out went nail polish and nylons. In came vitamins, nutritional supplements and a surgery center. "When a competitor introduced things we couldn't possibly keep in stock, we focused on service," Nicolais says. He also added more scheduled deliveries, began accepting credit cards and opened in-house charge accounts.

As a means of paying attention to his patients' personal health, Nicolais introduced counseling and drug information programs and is about to offer screening programs for osteoporosis and high cholesterol. More recently, Nicolais opened a card and gift shop down the street from Saxon. The two stores share a 20 person staff, borrowing shelf-stockers, sales help and delivery people as needed.

Most days, as soon as Nicolais arrives, he boots up the computers and listens to his voicemail messages. By 8:00am, he is already dispensing orders that have been recorded on email and voice mail. Throughout the day he will answer more than 100 consulting calls from patients, perhaps a dozen from physicians and scores from staff members within physicians' offices.

"As a community pharmacist and small business owner, I really have to focus on my patients and customers. I observe what's happening day in and day out and direct my attention to how to direct the flow of traffic for greater efficiency."

In addition to filling medication orders and talking with patients and physicians, Nicolais orders drugs, keeps records and spearheads the community outreach. If a customer comes in to sell an advertisement in a community newsletter — Nicolais is often the one to buy it. If a Girl Scout troop needs support, he is ready to give it. He also plans in-store wellness events for the community, such as smoking cessation programs.

Nicolais spends a good part of his day on the phone with insurance companies and managed care representatives to facilitate payments to patients and

"We have to allocate time to everyone because we are the patients' last safety valve — the most accessible member of the healthcare team. They know they can just walk through our doors, and we're always there to help them."

Jack Nicolais, RPh, MS

to Saxon. Sometimes payments take six to eight weeks to arrive and when they do, they're often for less than they were five years ago. As a result, a few years ago, Nicolais had to trim his professional staff and increase his own working hours. "It's been the main frustration in an otherwise idyllic profession," he says.

PATIENT POINT OF VIEW

An 85-year-old woman was receiving medications from many different physicians. The aide, with whom the woman lived, mistakenly assumed that they had coordinated her care plan and that her state of confusion was a natural byproduct of aging. Because Nicolais had known her for years, he was familiar with her conditions. He suspected the woman's worsening state of mind was the result of surfeit medications and called her aide and daughter in another state to discuss his observation. As result of his intervention, the daughter called the physician to request that her mother's daily medications be reassessed. Immediately, her mother's breathing, mental capacity and agility improved. "Sometimes just by knowing the customer, being supportive and explaining things to the caretaker, I have been able to help them. It's wonderful to be able to make a difference in someone's life."

>>> fast facts

What do you need?
- A desire to work extensively with people
- Education in business management (accounting, management, marketing, etc.)
- Courses in pharmacy administration may be helpful

What's it take?
- A current, active license to practice pharmacy
- Bachelor of Science (BS) or Doctor of Pharmacy (PharmD) degree*

Where will you practice?
- Community pharmacies (independent or chain)
- Supermarkets

*Students graduating after Spring 2004 will be required to have a PharmD degree

compounding pharmacist

A TRUE TALE

As a compounding pharmacist, Pat McGowen, BS, RPh, CDE, provides medications that either are not available through commercial channels or need to be prepared in different delivery forms. Sometimes he'll modify the taste to mask the bitterness for children. Other times he'll alter the mode of delivery. It is an important part of the pharmacy profession, which has its historic roots back as far as one can track.

McGowen's entry into the pharmacy field came after a five-year stint in the Navy as a hospital corpsman. It was right about the time he was discharged and considering what to do with his future that he ran into a friend who was at pharmacy school at South Dakota State University. The friend was enjoying it so much, and made it sound so appealing that McGowen considered the field for himself. After earning his bachelor's degree in pharmacy in 1982, McGowen took a job with a large medical center in Santa Maria, California. But after being there only four months, he was lured to Fair Oaks Pharmacy, a small store in a rural farming and ranching community on the ocean, just north of Santa Barbara. He is still there today.

In reflecting on his choice of profession, McGowen says it suits him perfectly. "My career is very satisfying, both professionally and socially," he says. "Working with people is a joy. And I love the small town atmosphere where everyone knows everyone."

Profiling the job

Some patients are allergic to preservatives or dyes or are very sensitive to standard drug strengths. As a result, their bodies are unable to tolerate generally accepted medications. When this happens, it is up to a compounding pharmacist to create a new formulation that will work well for the patient. Sometimes this can be done easily and other times the pharmacist will call on the physician for input. For example, formulations for those with

Compounding Pharmacist Checkpoint

Do you have curiosity and patience to try different things?

Do you have a good understanding of what people want and the creativity to deliver it?

Do you have strong interactive skills to explain your proposed alternative delivery systems and sell your concepts to patients and other health-care clinicians?

If so, read on

trouble swallowing can be changed from pill form to lollipop, topical gel or suppository. Even though compounding at Fair Oaks is limited to individual prescriptions, the pharmacy had initially invested $15,000 in chemicals and equipment to ensure its patients get exactly what they need.

Of the more than 300 prescriptions Fair Oaks handles each day, between four and five percent are personally compounded — four times the average rate in this country. This is in contrast to the 1930s and 1940s, when the rate of medicines compounded in pharmacies was as high as 60 percent. McGowen and the other staff pharmacists do all of the compounding. In addition, he manages the pharmacy diabetes program (he is a certified diabetes educator), and lectures nationally for several pharmaceutical companies.

"I don't try to duplicate what commercial drug manufacturers do," he says. "That's unnecessary and they've done tons of R&D work."

"If I had to name the one part of this job that I don't enjoy, it would be dealing with insurance companies." Sixty percent of his clientele either aren't covered by insurance or have to submit claims. "It means extra paperwork and phone calls and takes me away from doing what I'm trained to do, which is to be a pharmacist."

A day in the life

Fair Oaks Pharmacy is open from 9:00am to 6:00pm, but the pharmacists are on call 24 hours a day. Four pharmacists, including McGowen, rotate staffing the store. He estimates that each week he fields anywhere from three to 12 emergency calls, most of them coming from newly discharged patients. Although Fair Oaks has three delivery drivers and two vehicles, sometimes the demand is greater than the drivers can meet. Working with the owner pharmacist, McGowen and staff fill prescriptions and prepare new ones — breathing solutions, vaginal and rectal suppositories, topical creams, natural female hormone replacement preparation, and flavored oral medicines.

McGowen is constantly on the phone with physicians and nurses who have questions for him. "At least six times a day I am describing the optimal way to dose a new antibiotic or suggesting which foods will go with what compounds in order to avoid gastric upset." He adds that sometimes it is entirely up to him to determine how to deal with a patient, who may be abusing a medication.

> "One of my main goals is to work with the patients so they have a complete understanding of how to use their medications, how to store them, and what side effects they may experience."

McGowen, now 47, notices many more opportunities for pharmacists entering the field today than there were when he began compounding in 1983. And things keep changing for the better for both pharmacists and the people they serve. Much of this has to be credited to the pharmaceutical associations — both local and national. "Anyone who wants to effect change in his field must become active in the grassroots groups and the national associations," says McGowen. He also believes it is equally "important for a pharmacist to be a very visible presence in his or her community."

PATIENT POINT OF VIEW

"My five-year-old son goes on antibiotics periodically for recurrent ear infections. When he turned five, he started refusing to take any medicine. We tried to tell him how important it was, and of course tried a few little bribes, but no luck. And no matter what we tried to mix it in, he spit it out. Then, by good fortune, I walked into a small pharmacy and just happened to mention the situation to the pharmacist. He suggested I call my physician and get a prescription, which would allow him to compound the antibiotic into lollipop form. He also said he could add my son's favorite flavor. It actually worked! Now my son takes his medicine and I have a new pharmacist. Everyone is happier, including our physician."

Mrs. Barrie Levenson
New York, NY

"At least six times a day I'm describing the proper way to dose a new antibiotic or suggesting what foods with what compounds will avoid gastric upset or figuring out how to deal with a patient who's abusing medication."

Pat McGowen, BS, RPh, CDE

fast facts

What do you need?
- Advanced training in advanced compounding techniques
- Creativity and problem-solving skills
- Ability to work one-on-one with patients and determine individual needs

What's it take?
- A current, active license to practice pharmacy
- Bachelor of Science (BS) or Doctor of Pharmacy (PharmD) degree*
- Three-day course to teach special compounding skills

Where will you practice?
- Compounding pharmacies
- General pharmacies
- Hospitals
- Universities

*Students graduating after Spring 2004 will be required to have a PharmD degree

critical care pharmacist

A TRUE TALE

Critical care pharmacists are on the front lines of medical care, making life and death decisions at every turn. Often, they see the results of those decisions in short order. They go on patient rounds in the intensive care unit with a multidisciplinary team of health professionals, aiming to optimize the use of medications in the sickest patients in the hospital by identifying potential adverse effects and drug interactions. ICU patients take on average 10 different medications at any one time and the critical care pharmacist manages their total medication regime. They also provide information about the

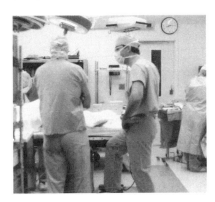

unique characteristics of drug response in critically ill patients, and because so little data exists on drug use in ICU patients, they often take an active role in doing research to fill this void.

Denise Rhoney, PharmD, had considered becoming a dentist before choosing pharmacy but soon realized that this was not for her. The 33-year-old native of Hickory, North Carolina, earned a Bachelor of Science in Pharmacy from the University of Kentucky College of Pharmacy in Lexington, Kentucky in 1990. In her last year of pharmacy school, she rotated through critical care and enjoyed its fast pace and the quick turnaround recovery of many patients. "It suited my personality," she says, "because I'm a quick talking Southerner."

Dr. Rhoney stayed at the University of Kentucky to receive her PharmD degree, and then began a residency in general clinical pharmacy, followed by a specialty residency in critical care at the Albert B. Chandler Medical Center there. She moved to the University of North Carolina at Chapel Hill in July 1993 for a two-year clinical research/drug development fellowship. Says Dr. Rhoney: "I have always had an interest in the brain and thought that a lot could be done to expand our collective knowledge in this area."

Critical Care Pharmacist Checkpoint

Would you feel comfortable dealing with comatose patients and their families?

Can you juggle and multi-task easily?

Are you good at prioritizing and managing time?

If so, read on

After her residencies and fellowships, Dr. Rhoney moved on to become a clinical instructor and professor at various other universities. Today she is both Assistant Professor of Pharmacy and Medicine in the Departments of Pharmacy Practice and Neurology at Wayne State University and works as well at Detroit Receiving Hospital.

Profiling the job

Dr. Rhoney is currently a neuro-trauma pharmacist in a 340-bed, all adult, Level One Trauma Center, meaning this hospital offers the highest level of care to trauma patients. Detroit Receiving Hospital includes a 92-bed emergency unit; ninety-eight percent of its admissions come through the emergency room.

The hospital is also a comprehensive stroke facility which takes referrals from other hospitals. Dr. Rhoney mentions there have been several significant advances in the field of stroke within the last five years. For example, a new agent that breaks up blood clots is now available for stroke patients (it used to be used strictly for heart patients). Dr. Rhoney explains that when a stroke patient arrives at the hospital, she and her team, which also includes a neurology and pharmacy resident, are summoned. She evaluates the patient to see if he or she is an appropriate candidate to receive the treatment. If so, she determines the dosage based on the patient's weight. A dispensing pharmacist prepares it and a nurse sets up an IV to administer it.

"There's no by-the-book approach to care here," says Dr. Rhoney. "Each patient is different and they're all so ill that the job requires a lot of thinking and creativity."

There are only a small number of neuro-trauma pharmacists in the country who work in both an intensive care unit and stroke pavilion. Other critical care pharmacists specialize in areas such as pediatrics, cardiac-thoracic, cardiology, general surgery, trauma, burns, and respiratory ailments. Detroit Receiving Hospital has seven pharmacists in critical care and three dispensing pharmacists available on a daily basis. Ninety percent of the patient population is indigent.

What Dr. Rhoney finds rewarding about her job is "helping to improve the care of patients in the ICU and seeing young minds grow and expand during the learning process. I see the light bulbs going on," she says. The gratitude she feels from the physicians who have come to rely on her more than makes up for any drawbacks, she says.

A day in the life

By 7:00am, Dr. Rhoney is at the hospital reviewing patient charts. A half hour later she begins rounds with the neuro-intensive care team. Visiting approximately 25 patients to examine and assess their care usually takes the team until noon.

Dr. Rhoney has minimal interaction with these patients, many of whom cannot speak, but talks to their families to learn about his or her medical history. Many patients are there as a result of alcohol, heroin, or cocaine involvement. Others are victims of assault, gunshots and car accidents. The others, stroke sufferers included, tend to be older.

After lunch, Dr. Rhoney follows up on any patient or situation that came up during rounds. She also checks on lab results or tracks down articles to educate physicians. She meets with the pharmacy students she's precepting (typically eight in a year) and goes over topic discussions and patient issues with them. In the latter part of the day, she attends to her research activities.

Dr. Rhoney currently has 10 active projects involving patients. One concerns the penetration of various drugs into the brain. (Recent research has led to a decrease in the duration of therapy of a seizure prophylaxis drug, resulting in fewer negative side effects.) Dr. Rhoney also has approximately a dozen academic articles in progress at any time and writes, on average, four grants a year. And she also ventures into the community to lecture on warnings and risk factors associated with stroke. "It's a big juggling act I play," says Dr. Rhoney, "but the advantage is, I am never bored."

Did you know?
A recent study showed that a group of ICU patients, with a pharmacist as part of the team, experienced 66 percent fewer adverse drug events (ADEs) and received better care than ICU patients not attended by a pharmacist.

PATIENT POINT OF VIEW

One Friday afternoon Dr. Rhoney was lecturing to her pharmacy students about stroke and its symptoms. Over the weekend, one attentive student recognized the symptoms in her husband and rushed him to the hospital. "What I learned from you in that class prompted me to seek medical attention for him immediately," the grateful student told Dr. Rhoney.

>> >> fast facts

What do you need?
- ○   ACLS (advanced cardiac life support) certification may be preferred
- ○   Ability to work as part of a multidisciplinary team
- ○   Ability to integrate patient care with teaching and research duties as well

What's it take?
- ○   A current, active license to practice pharmacy
- ○   Bachelor of Science (BS) or Doctor of Pharmacy (PharmD) degree*
- ○   General residency followed by a specialty residency in critical care

Where will you practice?
- ○   Intensive Care Units
- ○   Emergency departments
- ○   Operating rooms

*Students graduating after Spring 2004 will be required to have a PharmD degree

drug information specialist

A TRUE TALE

"I can honesty say I was not called to the specialty of drug information. I didn't even know I had a real calling to pharmacy for most of the time I was

in pharmacy school," says 34-year-old Kate Farthing, PharmD, a drug information pharmacist currently working at the Oregon Health Services University (OHSU) Hospitals and Clinics in Portland, Oregon.

Dr. Farthing grew up in small town in Kansas and attended the University of Kansas, earning her Bachelor of Science degree in Pharmacy in 1991. "I entered pharmacy school not knowing what pharmacy was all about," she says. "I chose it because I knew I had an interest in health care and medicine. Also, I wanted a degree I could turn into a specific job, rather than just having a chemistry or a microbiology degree and then wondering what I'd do with it. Still, it actually wasn't until I got into the last year of my undergraduate program, when clinical rotations began, that I knew I had made the right career choice."

That clinical rotation she refers to was her first and involved a six-week stint in a university teaching hospital. "I was lucky enough to be assigned to critical care. Being involved with patients and physicians and seeing how important a pharmacist is in direct patient care really sold me on the profession. I had been working at a retail pharmacy all through pharmacy school and enjoyed taking care of the outpatient issues. But working in the hospital, I saw a whole other side of pharmacy. What I saw was a far deeper connection to patients."

Farthing took a roundabout way to her Doctor of Pharmacy degree, but ended with the job of her dreams. She started with two years of undergraduate studies at the University of Kansas where her curriculum included most of the sciences and basic English. Then she applied and was admitted to the University of Kansas School of Pharmacy. Four years later, she graduated

Drug Information Specialist Checkpoint

Are you detail minded?

Are you patient and eager to keep digging beyond five or ten references?

Can you accept the fact that you may not always find an answer?

If so, read on

with a Bachelor of Science in Pharmacy, and then decided to obtain her Doctor of Pharmacy degree from Kansas. "A residency is generally not required after the PharmD," she says. "But if a pharmacy student is interested in specializing, or is in a hospital-based practice, that requires an extra year of training." Farthing selected this area because of the drug information pharmacist she worked with in her undergraduate and graduate training programs. "The woman was a true mentor to me. It was she who literally turned me on to drug information. I became her first resident," says Dr. Farthing.

In August 1994, Dr. Farthing arrived at OHSU in Portland as both an Assistant Professor of Pharmacy Practice and Director of the University's Drug Consultation Services. Since that time she has moved to the Department of Pharmacy Services as a drug information/drug policy pharmacist involved with shaping her department's plans for clinical pharmacy services. She also maintains the online formulary, helping decide what medicine physicians have access to within the 400-bed university teaching facility of OHSU. "If five drugs are available to treat hypertension, we evaluate them and then stock three," she says. "I need to be well versed in which are the most efficacious as well as cost effective to support the department's goal of maintaining a responsible drug budget."

Profiling the job

"There really is no standard job description for a drug information pharmacist," she says. Providing drug information means responding to questions and supporting a particular segment of hospital personnel — mostly physicians — in providing the best medical care through the use of drugs to patients. In other words, Dr. Farthing provides up-to-the-minute, in-depth information about pharmaceuticals to those who need and request it. The type of information called for depends on the individual practice setting. "My practice is at a university teaching hospital, so my questions are strictly from health care providers within my system. If you're a physician in a clinic affiliated with OHSU, you can call me or my service with drug-related questions and we find you the answers," continues Dr. Farthing.

Dr. Farthing notes that some people unfamiliar with this area of practice ask how it differs from, say, community pharmacy. The biggest difference is that, compared to a community pharmacist (or any hospital or chain pharmacist), a drug information pharmacist has dedicated time; time to explore and learn in depth about certain pharmaceuticals, time to read and review scientific literature, time to listen to drug company representatives, search the Internet, and determine what's really good and bad about a particular therapy. "Learning about new drugs as a practicing pharmacist is very different than studying drugs and drug classes in pharmacy school. If you have time, you read a journal article — usually just a news clipping that might say 'A new drug has been released, this is what it is, this is how it's dosed, these are its major side effects.' It might tell you a bit about the clinical trial conducted to garner approval from the Food & Drug Administration (FDA). And that's all the time you have," says Dr. Farthing. She adds, "It's necessary for a drug information specialist to know more information about a product than the average practitioner has the time or resources for. So I'll read on my own, or I'll hear about things from an FDA 'listserver' or a new approvals notification service that we subscribe to," she says. "Drug information specialists, as well as being practicing pharmacists, need to analyze what they are reading, process the information and then decide if it makes both common sense and clinical sense."

"My practice setting is actually different from other drug information pharmacists' who work in industry. For example, one of my residents went to work writing drug information-related materials for a publishing company. A former resident who focused on drug policy — something I also spend a lot of time doing — now works with a Medicaid program. My current resident has an interest in management, so we've structured his drug information training more around leadership and management-related activities."

Did you know? Drug information services are particularly important for problems involving the elderly, children or pregnant women.

A day in the life

Farthing arrives at the Drug Information Center by 7:30am each morning.
"Here I have computers, phones, and an excellent resource library at my
disposal. Part of my job is to be available to answer requests, so I begin
my day by checking my email to see if any new questions or responses to
outstanding questions or clarifications have come in."

Dr. Farthing says she can answer from 65 to 80 questions a month from
health professionals just within their system. Next she meets with residents
and students to determine what needs to happen that day. There may be a
resident and one to three students scheduled to work with Dr. Farthing in
the service. They begin by deciding who's doing what, who's working on
which questions, and who needs help. "We spend a lot of time talking about
the process of finding drug information. If someone is at the point where
they are ready to formulate a response to a question, we talk about their
search strategy, what they found and where they found it. I particularly
need to know they have dug into all corners of available literature to find
what they need." A sample question: can a specific drug cause a certain kind
of side effect? For example, can an antiviral drug cause thrombocytopenia?
Dr. Farthing says performing that research can be a whole day for a student.
Because she is on the hospital's Pharmacy and Therapeutics Committee,
Dr. Farthing must also weave into her day formulary meetings and meetings
about drug policy issues.

When time permits, even if it is just for a few minutes, Dr Farthing tries to
take time for reading new material. "It seems I'm always reading," she
explains. "I'm having lunch at the computer and reading press releases and
updates and whatever comes across my desk. I don't block out time to read,
I just find it."

Dr. Farthing doesn't see patients. Information reaches her by phone or
email, or by just asking the physician questions about particular patient. She
assesses functional capacity by asking: Can he clear the drug through his
renal system? How is her liver? What lab values are important? "In order to
respond to the physician's questions, I have to try and understand everything
about the patient. Since I don't interface directly with patients, that means I
have to be extra diligent in formulating the right questions for the physician
so I can paint an accurate picture and provide solid counsel."

PATIENT POINT OF VIEW

More drugs are always coming to market and the quality and quantity of information about each never stops. Physicians, nurses and other health care providers can't always keep abreast of what's happening on this front. They rely upon the drug information pharmacist to determine that the medications offered to patients will change their lives, save their lives or make their lives better.

fast facts

What do you need?

- Experience and/or training in clinical toxicology, poison, and drug information services
- Communication skills
- Ease with computers and other modern technologies

What's it take?

- A current, active license to practice pharmacy
- Bachelor of Science (BS) or Doctor of Pharmacy (PharmD) degree*
- One-year residency or other training in drug information pharmacy is preferred

Where will you practice?

- Hospitals
- Industry
- Community settings

*Students graduating after Spring 2004 will be required to have a PharmD degree

home care pharmacist

**Home Care
Pharmacist
Checkpoint**

Do you have
keen investiga-
tive skills?

Are you flexible
and able to
re-prioritize
quickly?

Are you
comfortable
working in
other people's
homes?

If so, read on

A TRUE TALE

Home care service is one of the fastest growing segments in the healthcare
arena as shorter hospital stays become ever more common. Home infusion

pharmacy is growing within home
care due to the demand for cost
effective methods when providing
long-term infusion therapies. Also,
there are humanistic considerations.
Typically more patients tend to
prefer to be treated at home rather
than in the hospital, because this
can be very helpful to recovery and
quality of life.

That's where home care pharmacists
like Tricia New, PharmD, FCSHP, come in. A native of Portland, Oregon,
New realized when she was a high school senior that she wanted a career
helping people and to be financially independent. She has done both since
graduating from pharmacy school.

After high school Dr. New immediately entered the pre-pharmacy program
at the University of the Pacific in Stockton, California and after completing
two years of pre-pharmacy course work, she earned her doctor of pharmacy
degree in 1984. After earning her PharmD, Dr. New completed a general
pharmacy residency at Good Samaritan Hospital in Portland, Oregon. As a
resident she developed a hospital-wide program to improve the handling
and disposal of chemotherapy, got a chance to be the acting Assistant
Director of Pharmacy, and was first exposed to home infusion pharmacy.
Thereafter, Dr. New completed a specialized pharmacy residency in hospital
pharmacy administration at Stanford University Hospital. At the time she
thought she wanted to be a Director of Pharmacy, but spent much of her
time that year developing the hospital-based home infusion program. This
made her realize she enjoyed the blend of clinical service, patient care, and
operational problem solving that is required daily in home infusion pharmacy.

Various stints over the next several years at other hospitals led her to her
current job: pharmacy manager of a Monterey, California-based home
infusion pharmacy. She is part of a multi-disciplinary team that includes
nurses, a dietitian, and support staff in areas such as reimbursement, techni-

cal, supply, delivery and clerical work. Dr. New directs the team in clinical monitoring and distribution services for patients in need of infusion and nutritional therapies. Other divisions of the company provide patients with beds and wheelchairs as well as dressing supplies and respiratory care needs.

Profiling the job

Dr. New is responsible for monitoring patients in need of infusion and nutritional therapy and making sure they receive the appropriate treatment. Patients may receive intravenous antibiotics, parenteral nutrition, chemotherapy, narcotics and inotropic agents (or any combination of the above). The management of these patients requires consideration of many different aspects of patient care including discharge planning, patient education, and the psychosocial needs of the patient. As patients are started on a therapy, it is necessary to evaluate if the patient or caregiver is capable of administering the medication. Other important questions the home care pharmacist should ask are: Will an infusion device be appropriate for the patient? Do they have adequate refrigerator storage for the medications? Are they able to understand how and when to contact the nursing and pharmacy services providing their therapies? "There's so much to factor in that's outside our control when you treat patients in their own homes," says Dr. New. "That means that when a patient calls to tell you something, you really have to listen very carefully because it may be the only evidence you have to go on. In home pharmacy the patient's self assessment is critical." Most of Dr. New's interaction with both nurses who make the home visits and physicians who oversee the program is handled over the phone. "If I'm not in front of my computer than I'm probably on the phone," says Dr. New.

At any given time, Dr. New's practice carries a census of around 200 home care patients, spread among four counties or a 90-mile radius. Dr. New treats everyone from newborns to geriatrics with a wide range of conditions that require infusion or nutritional therapy. Many patients are suffering from cancer or AIDS or long-term infections that have been treated with weeks of intravenous antibiotics. Some cannot eat because they are afflicted with Crohn's disease or other diseases that affect a patient's ability to adequately absorb nutrition. These patients require parenteral or enteral nutrition.

At one time, Dr. New used to visit some of her patients at home or in the hospital before discharge in order to teach them how to use the infusion devices and other equipment. Now, because of time pressures, she rarely

"Now, whenever I think my life is rough I remember my patients with cancer and AIDS and how brave they are and it just blows me away. They have taught me to value my own life more. But at the end of the day there's not a lot left of me. This is what I'm here to do."

Tricia New, PharmD, FCSHP

gets a chance to meet her patients and their families in person. "The reality is that while it may be the ideal, we can't personally meet every patient," she says. But she adds that she feels that her work empowers the patients she treats by giving them the choice to receive therapy and care in the home. "Sometimes it's letting them die with dignity surrounded by the people and place they love," says Dr. New. "And sometimes it's letting them mend in a more peaceful and pleasant environment."

A day in the life

Most mornings, Dr. New arrives at work at 8:00am and works until 5:30pm. She also rotates emergency coverage so that she is on call one or two nights a week and on Saturday or Sunday every other weekend. Twice a month she is called in after hours to enter and compound a prescription. Depending on the location she may also make the delivery.

Her first order of business is to review the compounding schedule for the day. She factors in laboratory results, updated patient information and will then have the pharmacy technicians compound the medication. Patient's pending discharge from the hospital, and new orders received during the night also need to be evaluated. Once the laboratory results have been obtained and evaluated, she begins to set up the specific ingredients.

At 9:00am and again throughout the day, Dr. New meets with nurses, a dietitian, pharmacy technicians and support staff to determine the plan for the day. Their discussion points include: medications being compounded for that day and the next day's delivery, pending referrals that need to be evaluated, and patients whose therapies are due to end soon. Throughout the day, working on the computer, she enters new prescriptions and order changes, evaluates laboratory results, makes

"You think you have a plan of care and then you discover circumstances change and the patient has additional needs," she says. "It's fair to say that in this job there is never a dull moment."

recommendations to physicians about therapy changes and documents her clinical notes into the patient's chart. She also checks the medications prepared by the pharmacy technician to verify that they are correct. By the time she finishes all this, it is late in the afternoon.

Since Dr. New started in home care, the therapies have also become more complicated. "It is not unusual for a patient to be taking more than one therapy at a time such as parenteral nutrition and intravenous antibiotics. Home care offers constant variety and intellectual stimulation," she says. "No wonder it is one of the fastest growing fields in today's health care environment."

PATIENT POINT OF VIEW

The patient was a three-year-old boy with a malignant brain tumor. Dr. New had been working very closely with his mother to help her manage the child's parenteral nutrition, antibiotics, and pain medications at home. Although they live an hour from her office, Dr. New made a patient visit and called frequently to make sure that they had everything they needed. As a result of the care provided by the home care team, the child was able to be with family, pain-free, until the end. After he died, the family thanked Dr. New for helping with the care of their son.

fast facts

What do you need?
- ○ Willingness to work as part of a multidisciplinary health care team
- ○ Effective communication skills
- ○ Strong record-keeping and documentation skills
- ○ Willingness to be flexible with hours and on-call

What's it take?
- ○ A current, active license to practice pharmacy
- ○ Bachelor of Science (BS) or Doctor of Pharmacy (PharmD) degree*
- ○ Intravenous experience preferred

Where will you practice?
- ○ Patients' homes
- ○ Home care agencies
- ○ Hospices
- ○ Specialized infusion companies
- ○ Ambulatory infusion centers

*Students graduating after Spring 2004 will be required to have a PharmD degree

chapter eight
hospice pharmacist

Hospice Pharmacist Checkpoint

Do you have good people skills and compassion?

Can you put aside what's "in the book" to focus on the person before you?

Can you deal with patients who are dying, and their families?

If so, read on

A TRUE TALE

The word "hospice" derives from the Latin word *hospitium,* meaning guesthouse, although the hospice is not a place. Eighty percent of hospice care is provided in the home and in nursing homes. One of the principle objectives of hospice care is to use modern pain management techniques to compassionately care for the dying. The first hospice in the United States was established in New Haven, Connecticut in 1974, by Florence Wald, a former dean of the Yale School of Nursing, and by her husband, Henry.[1] In its 30-year span of existence as a medical discipline, the role of the pharmacist in the hospice setting, like the hospice itself, has evolved. Today, many hospice pharmacists provide drug information services to patients and staff, act as members of the hospice

interdisciplinary team, monitor therapeutic outcomes, recommend drug therapies, and develop protocols for pain management as well as for specific symptom management such as nausea, vomiting, constipation secondary to opioid use, anxiety, agitation, excessive secretions, insomnia, depression, dyspnea, and thrush. A majority of hospice patients have cancer or long-term chronic illnesses such as heart failure or emphysema, and pain is the most common complaint. In fact, it has been estimated that 85 to 95 percent of pain syndromes, including severe forms, such as cancer related pain, can be adequately palliated using relatively simple techniques.

Alice Angelica Wen, PharmD, knew the Veterans Administration (VA) protocols long before she became a hospice pharmacist at the 220-bed VA hospital in Palo Alto, California. Her mother was a nurse at the Menlo Park VA campus when Dr. Wen was growing up. It was in 1993, after interning at that campus as an assistant to a long-term care pharmacist for the nursing home populace, that she realized that pharmacists provided more patient care than she had thought. Armed with this new appreciation, she directed her energies to the profession.

After earning a Bachelor of Science in biological sciences from the University of California at Davis in 1993, Dr. Wen moved on to the PharmD program at the University of Southern California School of Pharmacy in Los Angeles. She was the Outstanding Graduate of 1998.

During her four years in pharmacy school, Dr. Wen interned at the USC University Hospital inpatient pharmacy and in the Sav-On-Drugs store pharmacy summer internship program in 1996. Following graduation was a one-year residency in clinical pharmacy practice at Kaiser Permanente Hospital in Anaheim, California, where Dr. Wen worked in ambulatory care with patients suffering from such chronic diseases as diabetes, heart failure, asthma, hypercholesterolemia and hypertension.

Dr. Wen then went to Arcadia Methodist Hospital in Arcadia, California to pursue her interest in acute care medicine. As a clinical pharmacist there, she provided parenteral nutrition consultations, antibiotic dosing and anticoagulation monitoring while managing an intensive care unit satellite, transitional care units, and regular medicine flow. After three months though, she decided to move back to the San Francisco Bay Area to work at the VA Palo Alto hospital in its hospice/sub-acute department.

Profiling the job

The VA hospice department usually houses 22 to 25 patients. They are all terminal and their care is strictly palliative and pain management. The unit is open to all veterans and to some contracted nursing homes in the area. Medicare hospice eligibility depends primarily upon two factors: prognosis (as defined by Medicare) and goals of care. While a DNR status is not required for hospice admission, the goals of care should be primarily palliative. Many patients may not be able to meet Medicare eligibility on the basis of prognosis but may still have reasonable goals of care focusing on comfort. "Our goal is to keep the patient as comfortable as possible so they die with dignity and respect," says Dr. Wen.

She is also in charge of approximately 25 patients in sub-acute/long-term care, and is the sole pharmacist in both departments (she usually has a pharmacy resident and a fourth year pharmacy student during the school year to assist her). The sub-acute patients usually stay for six months to a year and may comprise those with post-surgery hip replacement, coronary bypass graft or even amputations that require rehabilitation. After two years,

Did you know?
There are approximately 500 hospice pharmacy consultants in the country.

Did you know?
There is no portion of caring for the terminally ill patient more important than pain management. As a result of implementing the concept of pharmaceutical care in the hospice setting, pain can be managed in an effective, compassionate way.

they're most likely transferred to nursing home units. Perhaps surprising for a VA hospital, many of the hospice patients are female and civilian. Their average age is 60, but Dr. Wen has recently had several women in their 40s and 50s, suffering from breast cancer. "In addition to pharmacological issues there are psychological, social and family issues to deal with," she says.

Hospice pharmacists work largely "behind the scenes" at the hospice agency offices or at a pharmacy under contract with the hospice to provide medications, including controlled substances for terminally ill patients. Because these patients are so ill, they are often on heavy doses of complicated medication regimens. Such a situation raises the possibility of harmful medication interactions.

"Someone asked me once, what it takes to do this job well. More than anything else, I think, it is the ability to enter deeply into the pain, suffering, and sadness that are a part of life and death and then to emerge on the other side into peace and joy. Over and over again."

Jim Hallenbeck, MD

For the hospice pharmacist, a big challenge to patient medication counseling is their fear of addiction — a fear which leads some patients to prefer to be in pain.

A day in the life

Dr. Wen is on the job by 7:30am Monday through Friday and works until 4:00pm. On weekends, another pharmacist covers, but Dr. Wen is nearly always reachable by pager. After routine chart review and preparation of formulas, around 9:30 each morning, Dr. Wen, along with a nurse practitioner or physician, meets with the night nurse to get caught up on each patient's changes. Usually, patients are more agitated at night than they are during the day. Then she visits each patient, and discusses adequate pain control and issues like thrush, diarrhea or constipation as well as pharmacological remedies. Dr. Wen also sees each newly admitted patient for a baseline evaluation.

By 11:00am, with recent lab results in hand, Dr. Wen and a pharmacy resident are in the long-term unit rounding with a physician and two nurse practitioners. Each cares for a dozen or so patients, looking for changes and side effects that may result from medications. Does it increase the patient's risk of falling? Is it leeching too much electrolyte from the system? Is the patient dehydrated? When problems exist, Dr. Wen will suggest alternative solutions. Then, complying with long-term care joint commission requirements, she writes her notes about each patient, explaining why a particular medicine is appropriate. The examinations and documentation usually take between two to three hours.

Dr. Wen also regularly confers with her pharmacy resident and three to four students. Every hour she verifies physician's orders to ensure the right drug has been prescribed for the right patient and that the right drip has been electronically entered.

Although the law currently stipulates that a pharmacist needs to visit hospice just once a month to review pharmacotherpy, Dr. Wen expects that as more people recognize the importance of pain management for the terminally ill, the demand for hospice pharmacists will soar.

The best thing about her job, she says, is dealing with her wonderful co-workers and patients. "We see them as friends. One of us will go buy a patient wine or ice cream. An occupational therapist celebrates happy hour every Friday with the patients. We try to make it as cheerful and home-like here as possible," says Dr. Wen. She concludes that it is hard losing people she's come to know and care about. Monthly grieving sessions led by a chaplain allow the staff to reflect on patients who have recently died. Dr. Wen also uses exercise to release stress.

At first, Dr. Wen balked at joining the hospice unit, fearful it would be routine and that she wouldn't learn new things. Now she's grateful she made that choice. "Many days I am so thankful for my life and health and that I can be part of caring, loving people who can provide a great environment," she says. "My experience has helped me realize that life is short and that I must make sure to have my affairs in order and my relationships with people in good standing."

"As a hospice pharmacist, I view the family as my patient. There's a need for me to talk with them and make them comfortable with the idea of opiates and morphine. Most people are adverse to it because they fear it will hasten their loved one's end. I explain how we're using the right amount to make the patient comfortable but not hasten death."

Alice Angelica Wen, PharmD

PATIENT POINT OF VIEW

The 41-year-old woman's breast cancer had metastasized and she had unresolved personal issues. Her relationships with her estranged husband and 16-year old daughter were bitter and her excruciating pain was only relievable for a short span with tremendous amounts of opiates. But when Dr. Wen talked to her, the pain that made her grimace and yell seemed to evaporate. She'd smile at Dr. Wen and tell her she enjoyed her company.

After three months on the unit, she died, but not before thanking Dr. Wen for feeding her meals, for spending time with her — for caring. After she was cremated the hospital held a service for her and her mother wrote a letter thanking the team for taking such great care of her, for making her comfortable and helping her move beyond constant pain to a better place.

>>> fast facts

What do you need?
- Compassion in counseling and educating hospice patients and their families
- Ability to work with a team of nurses, physicians, social workers, bereavement counselors, and volunteers
- Ability to give clear, precise directions and explanations to elderly patients
- Clear concept of appropriate pain management techniques and palliative care medicine

What's it take?
- A current, active license to practice pharmacy
- Bachelor of Science (BS) or Doctor of Pharmacy (PharmD) degree*
- Residency in Hospice may be preferred (especially for a practitioner without advanced degree training)

Where will you practice?
- Hospices
- Pharmacies under contract with hospices
- Patients' homes

*Students graduating after Spring 2004 will be required to have a PharmD degree

1 Yale School of Nursing. "Yale School of Nursing Convocation to Feature Hospice Founders and Noted Ethicist".

hospital staff pharmacist

A TRUE TALE

A few decades ago, hospital pharmacists were regarded as materials managers. They had little patient contact and worked deep in the depths of the hospital, away from the action. Today after an evolution which saw them shift their focus from the drug product itself to the quality of drug use and patients' health needs, they are key members of a multidisciplinary team. They advise on medication selection, administration and dosing, to assure optimal patient care, minimize a hospital's liability and control drug costs.

Hospital Pharmacist Checkpoint

Do you have leadership skills to work on a number of different committees, programs and tasks?

Are you motivated?

Are you comfortable with challenges and willing to make decisions?

If so, read on

As director of inpatient pharmacy services at Parkland Health & Hospital System in Dallas, Texas, Vivian Bradley Johnson, PharmD, MBA, FASHP, has always had a desire to help people. In the small town of Lake City, Florida, where she grew up, she knew the community pharmacist through church meetings and spoke at length with him about a career as a chemical engineer as compared to a career as a pharmacist. "He predicted that I would have many more opportunities to help people in pharmacy," she said.

Dr. Johnson, now 41, earned a Bachelor of Science in Pharmacy in 1982 from Florida A&M University in Tallahassee, and her PharmD degree from Mercer University Southern School of Pharmacy in Atlanta. In 1984 she did a residency in Clinical Pharmacy Services at the Veterans Administration Hospital in New Orleans.

Then it was on to Dallas's 964-bed Parkland Health & Hospital System, a tertiary-care, teaching healthcare system where she began as a staff pharmacist and became the coordinator for clinical services. As a clinical specialist in the Pharmacokinetics Service she monitored patient serum drug levels and assisted physicians in determining dosages and therapeutic efficacy of drugs with narrow therapeutic indexes. In addition to making rounds with the infectious disease medical staff, she developed a pharmacokinetics training program. From 1990 to 1993 as a Clinical Specialist of Investigational Drug Services in Parkland, Dr. Johnson opened the first pharmacy-based expanded access program in the AIDS clinic, assisted in establishing and chartering an investigational drug service networking group, acquired protocol funding from major pharmaceutical companies and managed the research and monitored all patients enrolled in these studies. For the next three years, as Assistant Director of Pharmacy Services, Dr. Johnson coordinated the delivery of medications and patient education throughout the hospital, developed initiatives to contain costs and promote efficiency, supervised staff and facilitated procedural modifications including the redesign of pharmacy services. Dr. Johnson conducted the pilot program for the Inpatient Discharge Medication Counseling Program and created and supervised the development of satellite services for pediatrics and surgery. She also developed procedures governing inpatient pharmacy services for Surgery, Medicine, ICU, Pediatrics, Neonatal, OR, and Oncology, and managed the space reconfiguration and development of the hospital's first IV clean room. She also assisted in the development of a computerized chemotherapy dose-checking program, supervised the implementation of an automatic dispensing machine program and initialized the hospital's first publication for chemotherapy and pediatrics. Along the way she earned an MBA from the University of Dallas.

Profiling the job

As director of all inpatient pharmacy related services at Parkland, Dr. Johnson supervises the oncology clinic and directs the activities of 120 pharmacists and technicians serving the medication and education needs of acute care, cancer patients and clinical research. She oversees patient-specific clinical services including reviewing patient charts, monitoring drug therapy and providing written follow-up to the prescribing physician. She also documents reports and manages adverse drug reactions, often evaluating the appropriateness of drug use and patient outcomes through a structured, ongoing process.

Other components to Dr. Johnson's job include budget development and management, liaising with senior management, the nursing staff and the medical staff, developing procedures and quality management indicators, implementing patient care services and pharmacy programs, recruiting and training staff, participating in quality assessments and evaluations, supervising patient education, monitoring support functions and developing long-range plans.

A day in the life

On some mornings, Dr. Johnson arrives at 6:30am to meet with physician specialty groups, one of approximately 25 meetings she has each week. She discusses with them any new initiatives or feedback from the programs she is monitoring. "Patient safety is a big issue in all healthcare organizations; the medical and hospital staffs are working on initiatives to prevent medication errors," she says. Otherwise, she is in by 8:00am, responding to emails and checking with managers to make sure the infrastructure is operating smoothly. If the computer systems are down and they can't do order entry, she leads the operation to determine how to care for patients despite that limitation. If the emails include requests for certain drugs not on the hospital's formulary, she'll get them evaluated and approved as a non-formulary agent or discuss with the Hospital's Pharmacy & Therapeutics Committee practitioners whether the drug should be added.

When she isn't in a meeting, Dr. Johnson is preparing for one or working on an assignment from another. She assists with developing the agenda for the Pharmacy & Therapeutics and Medication Use Cycle Subcommittee meetings, for example, and sets up resource initiatives for the hospital. Recently she oversaw the redesign of the oncology pharmacy process so patients can go to one place for all their medications and infusions instead of making multiple stops. She is also overseeing a new program to prevent recurrence of drug allergies, creating guidelines to counsel patients on what they received and giving them bracelets to remember what caused reactions.

Dr. Johnson automated drug distribution by installing machines on nursing units. Now pharmacists can review and evaluate the orders prior to entering them into the computer system and making the drug available. Three hours a week, she works with students and pharmacy residents. When she heads home to her own three young children at 6:00pm, she often carries along journals and reports.

"Initiating programs and making a lasting difference in people's lives is very rewarding and fulfilling," says Dr. Johnson. "Enhancing the oncology service was especially gratifying." Dr. Johnson also developed a Severe Drug Allergy Counseling by Pharmacists program and implemented a quality assurance process for anesthesia controlled substance accountability. Prior to the emergence of the Joint Commission on Accreditation of Healthcare

"Nothing is the same on any day here. You get experience and learn so much and feel good knowing that you're helping people."

Vivian Bradley Johnson, PharmD, MBA, FASHP

Organizations recommendations, she developed and implemented the action plan to remove potassium chloride concentrated injection vials from patient-care areas.

But she is often frustrated by "dreaming of things I want to do but can't because of the limitations of technology." For example, she is pressing for the development of a program whereby hand-held personal digital assistants are used to enter information during rounds and automatically generate a report.

PATIENT POINT OF VIEW

A 68-year-old woman who had been in the hospital for weeks finally died but the pharmacist's connection to the family didn't. Soon after, her son came back to tell the team how much his family appreciated all the help they gave his mother — not just the drug therapy but taking time to sit with her and talk about her life. "You were professional people," the son told her.

>>> **fast facts**

What do you need?
- Ability to work one-on-one with patients
- Organizational skills, to be responsible for systems which control drug distribution
- Proficient in math
- Good communication skills

What's it take?
- A current, active license to practice pharmacy
- Bachelor of Science (BS) or Doctor of Pharmacy (PharmD) degree*
- Technical specialization in a pharmacy field and/or management expertise may be required

Where will you practice?
- Hospitals
- Health systems

*Students graduating after Spring 2004 will be required to have a PharmD degree

chapter ten
industry-based pharmacist

A TRUE TALE

Dr. Sal Giorgianni's entry into the world of pharmacy was, as he calls it, "an accident," but a fortuitous one. "I was in high school and went to the

usual number of career fairs. I told a representative from one of the universities that I was interested in chemistry and biology and he suggested I consider pharmacy as a career that blended both. So I tried it. It was as simple as that."

Dr. Giorgianni attended Columbia University in New York City where he earned an undergraduate degree in pharmacy in 1973 and his Doctor of Pharmacy degree in 1975. He did an accredited American Society of Health System Pharmacists (ASHP) residency at New York's Lenox Hill Hospital. At Lenox Hill, during the early 1970s, he was a coordinator of clinical pharmacy services and specialized in pharmaceutical care in cardiovascular medicine and open heart surgery. During his school years, Dr. Giorgianni practiced community pharmacy, both chain and privately owned retail as an apprentice, intern and RPh. He was also Assistant Professor of Pharmaceutics and Adjunct Professor of Clinical Practice at Columbia University from 1973 until 1976.

Why did Dr. Giorgianni make the leap from a traditional practice setting to industry? "I had some friends who worked at Pfizer who loved industry and made it sound so appealing, I decided to give it a try," he says. His entry job at Pfizer Inc. in 1979, headquartered in New York City, was in the medical department where he coordinated the drug information program. He also took on additional responsibilties to manage some clinical trial programs. As he ascended the ranks at Pfizer, Dr. Giorgianni held a number of different positions, each offering a new and exciting opportunity while defining a particular area of industry. In describing his 22-year trip through the world of Pfizer, he says:

"From the medical department, I was appointed Associate Director of Training and Development for a sales division. I moved on to run some specialized professional educational programs and then went into the regulatory affairs department. My next job was in corporate strategic planning

Industry-Based Pharmacist Checkpoint

Are you interested in working in a business environment?

Are you willing to work long hours in exchange for a broad opportunity to move up the ranks?

Do you have or are you willing to pursue good credentials in business?

If so, read on

and policy, which transitioned into regulatory, researched healthcare policy and corporate strategic business planning. Then, through various reorganizations, I came into my current responsibility as Director of External Relations for Pfizer Pharmaceuticals Group where I have been happily ensconced for the past four years."

Profiling the job

Industry pharmacy is extremely broad. Within the pharmaceutical world, there is vast opportunity. Industry pharmacists need a pharmacy degree and can be involved in everything from sales to research to law to marketing to general business. "However, to move into specialty areas, one needs experience and training, and must really excel," says Giorgianni. "For example, a pharmacist wanting to go into marketing needs a top tier MBA level education and background in marketing before moving up the ranks. A pharmacy degree is a wonderful entry point  but it's up to him or her to develop business skills." Departments within Pfizer open to pharmacists include:

○ Pharmaceutics: develop new drugs and novel dosage forms.

○ Research development: work in any capacity from bench scientist to clinical research specialist, conducting and managing clinical trials.

○ Field investigation: develop and administer drug trials.

○ Epidemiology: monitor and manage safety reporting for drug products and new product portfolios.

○ Production: work in both early production development and quality control responsibility.

○ Regulatory affairs: work with the U.S. Food and Drug Administration (FDA) on regulation of drug development and promotion.

○ Medical and scientific information: work as a drug information specialist for industry.

- Education: develop programs to enlighten professionals on uses and efficacy of specific drugs.

- Sales: sell in the field or work with special high profile clients and large institutions.

- Marketing: work on advertising and/or general marketing of products.

- Finance: work with business issues and company financials.

- Legal: work in all aspects of law, from contract law to malpractice to regulatory law.

- Lobbyist: work on Capitol Hill or on the state level to forward industry and corporate concerns.

Dr. Giorgianni describes working in industry as professionally satisfying and financially rewarding. Most pharmaceutical companies strive for entry-level salary parity with other business environments. But once a pharmacist starts building his or her career — especially as they develop further credentials, specialization and expertise — there is a fairly unlimited salary potential, he says.

One plus of working in the pharmaceutical industry — especially if it's a global organization — is the flexibility, latitude and opportunity that comes with travel and moving around the world. Many industry pharmacists find themselves working in both domestic and international divisions, which includes multi-level travel. "At Pfizer, our obligation is to provide scientifically sound information that fits the healthcare needs of a particular country or environment. To this end, we have teams of pharmacists, physicians, PhDs, and biomedical scientists whose job it is to help these entities organize and manage the information exchange between our corporation and their practicing scientists and others," says Dr. Giorgianni.

Industry pharmacists rarely have patient contact. Within the drug information department, some pharmacists do provide answers to patients' questions (that come in by phone or mail) about products, their use and side effects. Other pharmacists are responsible for managing clinical trials but they don't interact with patients or counsel them, even indirectly. "Still," Dr. Giorgianni says, "that doesn't mean we aren't practicing our profession. Like academia, industry is a specific branch of pharmacy practice. In both fields, we may not see patients every day but we are still practicing pharmacists."

Did you know?
Research and development spending by pharmaceutical industries has risen from about $2 billion in 1980 to about $24 billion in 2000, an estimated 20 percent of total revenues. Pfizer will annually invest about $5 billion in its research efforts in 2002.

As Director of External Relations, Dr. Giorgianni is responsible for a department that represents Pfizer to a range of professional, voluntary health and academic organizations and institutions. He is also responsible for helping develop and craft Pfizer's policies regarding healthcare delivery, research and regulatory policy. The overall objective, he says, is to work together with external groups and individuals outside Pfizer "to create a healthcare business environment that serves patients well and is mutually rewarding."

Also under Dr. Giorgianni's purview is publishing The *Pfizer Journal*. This corporate bimonthly contains articles on biomedical research and healthcare issues by noted experts. It is distributed to academicians, government officials and others in the healthcare delivery industry.

Dr. Giorgianni is one of the co-developers and managers of the Pfizer Clinical Trials Skills Development Program, which trains scientists throughout the world in the methods of clinical trial investigation. A team of PharmDs, PhDs, and MDs — all specialists in research — present this program in countries where such skills are generally not taught. "Thousands of clinicians and academicians overseas — particularly younger ones — are drawn to clinical research and want to become involved in it as part of their career," he says. "However, half a dozen universities at best actually teach advanced research skills as part of their pharmacy, nursing, medicine or dentistry curricula. So we go in and offer it ourselves. It's useful for the students, clinicians, the university, and it also benefits Pfizer by helping us work with better trained researchers. This is essential since advanced research is a core attribute of our contribution to society and as a successful business."

A day in the life

Ask a pharmacist to produce an hour-by-hour log of a typical day and he or she will tell you it's almost impossible. It is probably even harder for an industry pharmacist because careers that fall under the umbrella "industry" are so varied. Someone working in medical information, for example, has day-to-day responsibilities and objectives that are very different from a pharmacist in the legal department. Even from company to company, the same job title may describe a very different range of responsibilities for the pharmacist.

All pharmacists practicing in industry have one thing in common, however: They all work hard and they work long hours. "Students sometimes want to go into industry because they're looking for a good 9-to-5 job. There is no such thing," says Dr. Giorgianni. "If you're dedicated to building and developing a career within the business environment, you can't do that and still walk out the door at five o'clock."

Dr. Giorgianni can begin his day just about any time — and often does, since he is usually on the road and may wake up in a different time zone every day. That takes getting used to, he says. "Fifty to 70 percent of my time and a large part of my staff's time is spent away from Pfizer headquarters, meeting and working with various companies, organizations and academic institutions and their leaders to identify their business needs and discuss partnership opportunities with Pfizer. I'll travel to their organization's headquarters or to special meetings at off-site conferences. The remainder of my month is spent at Pfizer's New York offices, working to identify and strategize our corporate needs."

Dr. Giorgianni's department is responsible for liaising with general medical, pharmacy, nursing, physician assistants and other healthcare practitioner groups. Prominent among these are the American Society of Health System Pharmacists (ASHP), American Pharmaceutical Association (APhA), American Academy of Family Physicians (AAFP), American Academy of Physicians Assistants (AAPA) and American Academy of Nurse Practitioners (AANP).

Much of Dr. Giorgianni's time with APhA and ASHP is spent trying to understand the needs and issues currently facing practicing pharmacists

"You can get an industry job with basic pharmacy credentials but if you want to build a long-lasting, sustainable and flexible career, you need to develop both formal, business and on-the-job credentials. The requirements for building an industry career in pharmaceutical law are quite different from building a career in epidemiology. Each needs a different advanced degree and a different set of work experiences."

and developing programs or partnerships within Pfizer to address these issues. This wide variety of issues includes everything from providing drug distribution monitoring to developing programs to enhance clinical practice skills. Meetings with pharmacist groups provide Dr. Giorgianni and his team with the information and feedback Pfizer needs to properly address their needs. Pfizer has 96,000 employees around the world.

>>> ## fast facts

What do you need?
- ○ Ability to meet technical demands and perform scientific duties
- ○ Administrative, management, and/or business skills may be useful
- ○ Sales and/or marketing skills may be useful
- ○ Excellent communication skills

What's it take?
- ○ BS, MS, PharmD, MBA or PhD in a technical discipline*
- ○ Experience in the discipline of interest
- ○ Exceptional credentials for those interested in the research area

Where will you practice?
- ○ Pharmaceutical companies
- ○ Biotechnology companies

*Students graduating after Spring 2004 will be required to have a PharmD degree

infectious disease pharmacist

A TRUE TALE

Robert C. Owens, Jr., PharmD, is a Clinical Instructor at the University of Vermont College of Medicine and Clinical Specialist in Infectious Disease at Maine Medical Center in Portland. One thing practice has taught Dr. Owens is that infectious organisms, or "bugs," are smarter than humans. "Of course, when every twenty minutes a new generation is born, it makes it easy to take advantage of Darwinian selective pressure and employ survival advantages," says the 34-year-old clinical pharmacist.

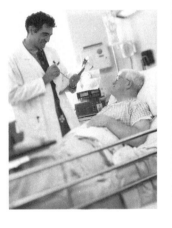

Although Dr. Owens was born in Maine where he now practices, he has lived in nine different states. It is difficult to say exactly where his interest in pharmacy originated, but he says it was probably somewhere between mixing items from the medicine cabinet in the bathroom sink as a child and nearly blowing up his college chemistry laboratory during an experiment. Nevertheless, having an organic chemistry professor at the University of Tennessee in Knoxville who was originally a pharmacist certainly confirmed his interest in the profession. Throughout his undergraduate lectures, this professor would often discuss pharmaceuticals as examples of various principles.

After the University of Tennessee, Dr. Owens enrolled in the Mercer University School of Pharmacy in Atlanta where he received his PharmD degree. For the next year, he did a clinical pharmacy practice residency at DeKalb Medical Center in Atlanta followed by a two-year infectious disease fellowship at Hartford Hospital in Hartford, Connecticut. In 1997 Dr. Owens moved to Delaware's Christiana Care Health System, as a clinical pharmacy specialist in infectious disease. Here Dr. Owens directed the antimicrobial management program, conducted clinical research, and taught students from two nearby pharmacy schools on infectious diseases rotations. A year later he joined Maine Medical Center in Portland as its infectious disease clinical pharmacy specialist.

Infectious Disease Pharmacist Checkpoint

Are you detail oriented?

Are you prepared for long hours and demanding situations?

Are you persistent?

If so, read on

Did you know?
Malaria, a leading parasite killer of children in developing countries, affects up to 500 million people across the globe and kills one person every 10 to 15 seconds. Tuberculosis trails only lower respiratory infections and HIV/AIDS as an infectious cause of death. The TB bacterium currently infects one-third of the world's population, and eight million people develop disease symptoms each year.

Profiling the job

At his 550-bed community teaching hospital, Dr. Owens is responsible for managing the pharmacotherapy for patients with infectious diseases as well as teaching clinicians rational approaches to selecting anti-infective agents in the battle against infectious diseases.

In addition to his clinical duties, Dr. Owens also works with compassionate use programs offered by the pharmaceutical industry to provide novel investigational treatment options for infections where traditional treatment has failed or is not well tolerated by the patient.

Maine Medical Center serves the entire state of Maine and parts of Massachusetts and New Hampshire. Dr. Owens sees a variety of infections in this region of the country. Most are similar to common but serious infections found all around the United States such as pneumonias, endocarditis, osteomyelitis, and infectious complications resulting from cancer chemotherapy. Zoonotic infections (or animal-transmitted infections), such as lyme disease and human granulocytic erlichiosis are found here more commonly than in some other parts of the U.S.

"Common infections such as pneumonia, have become difficult to treat. Some of these organisms are resistant to the most traditional therapies and resistance to multiple antibiotics is continuing to rise."

Being on the front lines of infectious disease means there's never stagnancy and always opportunity for learning. "The CDC is instrumental in identifying and containing infection throughout the world. But despite such global efforts, nature is very persistent. I believe it is only a matter of time before a previously rare infectious entity appears in the U.S.," says Dr. Owens. On the other hand, he continues, it is the more common infections that pose the largest threat because they have developed resistance to currently available antibiotics.

A day in the life

Soon after he arrives at 7:30am, Dr. Owens makes rounds with the infectious disease teaching team comprised of an attending physician, a physician fellow, two medical residents and a medical student. For three to four hours, the group sees between 20 to 25 patients, many of whom are critically ill. Dr. Owens is responsible for selecting the most effective drugs and dosage for each patient's infection and for monitoring any adverse events.

During the rest of his day, Dr. Owens sees patients as part of an antibiotic management program that was launched in 2001. First he and a physician review a list of patients on antibiotics who are not being seen by the infectious disease service. In the afternoon he screens the records of 50 to 60 in-hospital patients for drug appropriateness and follows up with visits to another 25.

For 30 percent of the patients he reviews, he suggests change, most often because patients are on antibiotics when they are no longer required. In other cases the dose needs to be optimized or therapy is duplicated.

By mid-afternoon, Dr. Owens is often either attending a committee meeting or preparing for one. He's on the Medical Center's Medication Use Evaluation, Cystic Fibrosis, Pharmacy and Therapeutics, Infection Control, and Adverse Drug Event Committees. He also uses this time to prepare pharmacology lectures which he delivers three times a week to residents, faculty and fellows. He's involved in one of several ongoing pharmacokinetic or pharmacodynamic studies that involve volunteers, clinical patients, animals and in-vitro laboratory studies. He usually doesn't leave the hospital before well into the evening, carrying home journals to read and manuscripts to write. "This is definitely not a nine-to-five job," says Owens.

Dr. Owens has presented at numerous grand rounds and participated in international presentations on drug-resistant organisms, pharmacoeconomics and antibiotic selections to treat various infections. He has studied and written a number of articles regarding new antimicrobial agents, bacterial resistance, pharmacokinetics and pharmacodynamics, and the appropriate use of antibiotics. In addition, he has lectured extensively on these topics at both national and international meetings. He also serves as a reviewer for several journals and is on editorial boards as well.

"Bacterial superbugs tend to slip around our efforts to wipe them out. These pathogens were here long before we were, and will remain long after we are gone."

Robert C. Owens, Jr., PharmD

There is not a lot of long-term patient contact, as most of the patients he sees are acutely ill and require immediate attention. "Fortunately, most of our patients ultimately improve on therapy. Many are completely cured after treatment with antibiotics, which is the most rewarding aspect of my job."

PATIENT POINT OF VIEW

Every now and then, there are patients who require long-term follow up for infections that may require up to a year of antibiotics to cure. One man required a year of therapy after his release from the hospital. Because the patient lived far from a medical treatment facility, Dr. Owens personally delivered his treatments to him. The patient's family was grateful for the medication and for the questions about therapy that Dr. Owens was able to answer for them.

>>> # fast facts

What do you need?
- Ability to work one-on-one with individual patients, pharmacists, physicians and other clinicians
- Ability to conduct general antimicrobial drug reviews and participate in the development of antimicrobial drug use policies
- Research skills
- In-depth knowledge of antimicobial pharmacology

What's it take?
- A current, active license to practice pharmacy
- Bachelor of Science (BS) or Doctor of Pharmacy (PharmD) degree*
- General residency and/or fellowship training in infectious diseases highly recommended

Where will you practice?
- Research settings
- Hospitals
- Universities
- Government

*Students graduating after Spring 2004 will be required to have a PharmD degree

long-term care pharmacist

A TRUE TALE

In her sophomore year at Clemson University in Clemson, South Carolina, Renee Jarnigan, RPh, had an epiphany. An undeclared liberal arts major interested in education and teaching, the 30-year-old native of Blythewood, South Carolina woke up one day and knew she wanted to be a pharmacist. "I'd worked at my home town pharmacy throughout high school and during my college summer break and suddenly, one day during my sophomore year, I discovered I missed working there and the contact with the public it offered me," she says.

Clemson didn't have a pharmacy program, so Jarnigan transferred to the Medical University of South Carolina Pharmacy School in Charleston. Three years later, she graduated with a Bachelor of Science in Pharmacy degree.

Her first job was at a pharmaceutical care software company, CarePoint Inc., in Charleston, where she trained community pharmacists on how to use their proprietary software to assist in the management of patients' disease states. The software enabled pharmacists to more efficiently document their services and be compensated for their time, instead of being compensated just for the product. In January 1999, after a five-year stint, she moved to Network Healthcare in Greenville, a five-year-old long-term-care dispensing and consulting pharmacy serving 2,200 residents in nursing and assisted-living facilities. Currently, Network Healthcare employs nine pharmacists, five of whom dispense drugs and four, including Jarnigan, who do consulting.

Profiling the job

At Network Healthcare, Jarnigan is responsible for a roster of 15 different assisted-living and skilled nursing facilities with a census of over 800 patients. As a consulting pharmacist governed by federal regulations, she is required to come in monthly to review every drug each patient in her populace is receiving in the skilled nursing facilities. This is not yet a requirement in the assisted-living setting, although a few choose to have this service as well.

It's rare for a patient in a long-term facility not to be taking some kind of medication. Because it makes dispensing so much easier and safer, there is

"I like working with the elderly. I have a lot of respect for their intelligence and for what they have seen and lived through. Dealing with these particular residents is a joy — even the ones with less patience."

Renee
Jarnigan, RPh

an emphasis on providing medications in a prepackaged form. Still, the pharmacy maintains an open formulary, giving numerous prescribing options to the many physicians who write prescriptions.

Each year Network Healthcare pitches to renew its annual contract. "We are not the least expensive but we're probably the most service-oriented," boasts Jarnigan. That service component includes developing wellness programs for residents in the assisted-living facilities that also involve family members. For example, since more than a third of her population have osteoporosis and are on calcium and vitamin D supplementation, they coordinated an osteoporosis workshop to discuss the disease and medications to stop bone loss and promote regeneration. The pharmacy also offers an immunization program, which was developed by Jarnigan and her colleagues. Last year they administered 800 flu shots, all of which were paid for by Medicare. "These programs give us hands-on time with the residents and let them see what pharmacists can do for them other than dispense drugs," she says. Jarnigan is also involved with training staff of the facilities about different diseases and how to give insulin injections, use glucometers and understand a bit more about disease progression and sufficient monitoring. "If a staff member understands these diseases better, he or she can identify or handle a small problem before it becomes bigger," she says.

A day in the life

Jarnigan usually arrives at her office around 8:00am and immediately begins to review her day planner. One recent day she drove 120 miles, visiting three different facilities. She totes a reference manual, a laptop computer and a portable printer to look up drug information and record notes when she needs to. At the residences, she conducts in-service training sessions with staff, reviews charts and physicians' and nurses' notes, meets with utilization committees comprised of the medical director and nurses, and sees patients. Usually she visits just one facility a day but if they're small, she can get to two. Then Jarnigan returns to the office to finish her paperwork, return phone calls and schedule in-service offerings. By the end of a 45- to 48-hour week Jarnigan is "pretty much wiped out," she says.

Jarnigan is on salary but notes, "I don't do this job just for the money, but also for the personal reward. I like working with the elderly. I have a lot of respect for their intelligence and for what they have seen and lived through. Dealing with these particular residents is a joy — even the ones with less patience."

Jarnigan also enjoys contact with all levels of the medical profession. Physicians, nurses, administrators and staffers at the residences generally welcome her assistance. "Physicians have so many patients to diagnose and provide treatment plans for, they are increasingly starting to rely on pharmacists to assist with drug management. That is what we're trained to do."

For facility staff, new technologies predict an exciting future. Automated med-carts provide accurate dispensing by staff; electronic medical records help with documentation of care and allow pharmacists to have more time for consultation projects. As centralized medical records databases become increasingly available, staffers can punch in a patient's ID and the computer will produce a list of the medications he or she is to take. This is better than pouring over paper records says Jarnigan, because it takes care of documenting the transaction on the patient's record while providing pharmacists with more time for consultative practice.

Jarnigan admits that life on the road can sometimes be trying. Some cold, rainy days she simply doesn't want to drive. Sometimes she's away a week each month at the most distant facilities. Her husband, whom she met at her first job, is a pharmacist for a software company. "I joke with him about having 'bankers hours'," says Jarnigan, "but he works hard and has long days just like I do." But then she reminds herself that every day on her job something happens that's rewarding: a drug therapy has been changed and a patient flourishes; or she had good communication with a physician and they accomplish something important, working together as a team.

"It's easy for people who work in long-term care to lose sight of what the patient was like at a younger age. Some of our residents were accomplished musicians or noted engineers. I always try to recognize my patients' contributions and, of course, treat them with dignity. This job is all about reinforcing the golden rule."

"Working in long-term care makes me more aware of aging in general," says Jarnigan. "The sad side of this job is seeing some residents who do not get visitors and of course, I think, that could be me in their place. And then I am determined to give them as much as I can, starting with a smile."

Did you know?
The number of seniors needing long-term care is projected to rise to 13.8 million by the year 2030; 5.3 million will reside in nursing homes and other long-term care facilities.

PATIENT POINT OF VIEW

A 90-year-old resident of an assisted-living center had osteoporosis, hypertension and diabetes, and was taking her own treatments. Jarnigan interviewed her and went over her medications. Afterwards she prepared a folder in large print type with all the information they'd discussed plus possible side effects of the drugs. These were easier to read than the standard flyers usually stacked at the pharmacy. During the interview process the woman kept repeating "Oh, I didn't know that." Several months later Jarnigan spoke with the women and learned that she had been to a medical appointment. During the appointment, the physician wanted to stop one medication to start a new one. The patient, remembering the discussion with Jarnigan, asked the physician if she should stop the medication right away. The physician consulted some references and changed his recommendation so that the antihypertensive drug would be tapered rather than stopped all at once.

>>> fast facts

What do you need?
- Good communication skills and ability to interact well with people
- Ability to work as part of a healthcare team
- Must enjoy working with a geriatric community

What's it take?
- A current, active license to practice pharmacy
- Bachelor of Science (BS) or Doctor of Pharmacy (PharmD) degree*
- Certification in geriatric pharmacy is preferred
- One-year residency in geriatric pharmacy is preferred
- Clerkships in long-term care may be helpful

Where will you practice?
- Nursing homes
- Hospitals
- Assisted-living facilities
- Psychiatric hospitals
- Home care
- Subacute care facilities

*Students graduating after Spring 2004 will be required to have a PharmD degree

managed care pharmacist

A TRUE TALE

Steven Vollmer, RPh, was born and raised in Harvey, North Dakota. The 37-year-old pharmacist still refers to his hometown of 2,500 people as "a one-stoplight town." Even in his younger years, Vollmer had an affinity for the health profession. "It is a reflection of the way I was raised by my

parents," he says, "They were always quite open to helping people." In high school, when he started looking for a college to attend, he knew that his profession would be medically based. "I wanted to do something where I could help people and see the results. In health care, you have a direct impact on the lives of your customers. You do your job well, they do better and you see it." Because of his interest in chemistry, pharmacy appealed to Vollmer. He was also looking for a lifestyle "that would support where I saw myself in ten to twenty years." That meant raising a family and spending time with them. "Pharmacy gave me an opportunity to work with people, help them, and see my efforts rewarded on many levels. At the same time, it offered a lifestyle he liked, with no 'on call' schedule."

Vollmer went to North Dakota State University School of Pharmacy. In his senior year, representatives from many of the area's chain pharmacies came to campus to recruit, and he joined a chain that seemed to offer the work environment he sought. After one year on the job there he left for a smaller chain in hopes of spending less time dealing with third-party paperwork and gaining a more flexible work schedule. Unfortunately, the small chain went out of business so Vollmer then joined Kaiser Permanente, to be a staff pharmacist. "I have to admit, I loved the idea of being in managed care. Specifically, not worrying about the multitudes of insurance companies, but rather spending more time with patients really appealed to me. We don't get involved in all the nuances of different insurance companies, in effect, we *are* the insurance company." Vollmer says that for him, that was a major difference between dispensing for a managed care pharmacy and dispensing

Managed Care Pharmacist Checkpoint

Are you good at directly accessing and interpreting medical information on large numbers of patients?

Are you good at building relationships?

Do you prefer working in a medical center type of environment?

If so, read on

"Managed care pharmacy, as well as most other areas of pharmacy, is a different world today than it was fifteen years ago. With access to the Internet and other educational materials, our members are generally much better educated about their medical problems as well as the drug therapies they are on."

for a chain. "Chains deal with hundreds of different insurance companies, we deal with one — our own. Of course, the clinical aspect is remarkably different as well," Vollmer adds.

After two years as a staff pharmacist at Kaiser, Vollmer became an assistant pharmacy manager for one of their larger medical centers in the division. Six months later he was promoted to Director of Pharmacy Operations for their Springfield Medical Facility where he worked for four years before being promoted to his current position of Director of Pharmacy Operations for the Falls Church Medical Facility.

Profiling the job
Medical facilities within the Kaiser Permanente Central East Division offer different services depending on the facility's size and membership base. The Falls Church facility supports approximately 75 providers and offers a full range of medical services including adult primary care, pediatrics, family practice, obstetrics/gynecology, and urology, pulmonology, ENT, ophthalmology, dermatology, podiatry, orthopedics and gastroenterology. It is also an urgent care center where, after 5:00pm, other staff arrive, including physicians, pharmacists, nurses, and lab personnel. "It becomes like an emergency room center where our members can obtain medical care into the evening and throughout the night," says Vollmer.

Vollmer calls the pharmacy at Kaiser a cross between a chain pharmacy and a hospital pharmacy. Like chain pharmacies, Kaiser pharmacies sell OTC products, dispense drugs in non-unit dose packaging, and work with cash collection at the service windows. With respect to hospitals, Kaiser pharmacies do some IV work, have access to the complete medical picture of the patient when necessary, and have direct access to 80–90 percent of the prescribers because they reside in the same building. The ability to review a patient chart or the most recent ordered labs is comparable; yet the hospital patient may stay for only days or weeks, whereas the Kaiser patient may be served for years. As Vollmer explains, "It is due to this integrated healthcare system that Kaiser's pharmacies are clinically oriented. The pharmacist can have a more direct impact on patient care. For instance, when appropriate to patient care need, we can use our computer system or paper medical records to access patients' lab values and providers' progress notes. "Our in-house providers can access the pharmacy records, of course, as well," Vollmer says.

Vollmer commends the philosophy behind the Health Maintenance Organization (HMO). "Whereas retail pharmacies make money when more prescriptions are filled, an HMO makes money when patients require less medical appointments, procedures, and prescriptions. What more would you want?" Vollmer asks. "We, for example, work to keep our patients well-immunized not only because it's cost effective, but even more so because it's the right thing to do ethically for the health of the communities in which we reside. We all feel good about that."

Another upside Vollmer points out is that Managed Care Organizations have the capability to provide tremendous professional diversity for their pharmacists. At the Kaiser Falls Church pharmacy we offer disease state and medication management clinics, "Our pharmacy offers both an anticoagulation and diabetes clinic as well as a cholesterol treatment program. In our anticoagulation clinic, we have three full-time pharmacists plus a full-time pharmacy technician working with the roughly 1400 patients taking anticoagulants across all eight of our northern Virginia medical centers. These pharmacists work directly with patients, while staying in continuous

Did you know?
The earliest
HMO originated
in 1929 at the
request of the
Los Angeles
Department
of Water
and Power.

contact with their providers, to keep the patients within the therapeutic "international normalized ratio" or "INR" goal. On the other hand, the diabetes clinic is more multidisciplinary in approach because four different provider types work to manage the care of these patients and for example, to ensure the hemoglobin AIC is within an acceptable range."

A day in the life
The daily responsibilities of a pharmacist working in the Kaiser Falls Church Medical Center pharmacy vary. Their 40-hour weekly schedule translates to four 10-hour days. Each day is different — and it's designed that way. The full time pharmacists can rotate through up to four of six areas each week, which include the dispensing operations, the anticoagulation clinic, the diabetes clinic, the lipid service, the pharmaceutical care service and a "drug information" type area for both physicians and patients.

For a pharmacist to practice in most of these areas, he or she must first successfully complete an 8-week training program, and also demonstrate competency with all the necessary skills and needed knowledge base. By the time they're through, Vollmer says, they are not only highly knowledgeable in the subject at hand, they're also skilled in performing patient interviews and assessment work. The upside of this situation is that the pharmacists have both an opportunity to learn new skills and experience much diversity within their work environment while the organization benefits from both better pharmacist recruitment and retention. The patients benefit too because they have access to highly trained and knowledgeable pharmacists at service areas. As a result of this rotational schedule, a day in the life of a managed care pharmacist at Kaiser Falls Church depends on the clinic to which that pharmacist is trained and assigned. Within the clinics arena, the pharmacist generally reviews both lab work and progress notes from the previous day, contacts the patient when additional information is needed, and makes some therapy decisions while in communication with the provider. Additionally the pharmacist will assist in maintenance of the electronic patient database, answer patient calls into the clinic, and occasionally see new patients initially in a class setting.

PATIENT POINT OF VIEW

'It may sound odd, as the Director of the Pharmacy, the people I get to know best are the ones who complain the most. When they have issues or they can't get ongoing satisfaction through regular channels, they come to me. I am usually able to help them out. One particular man comes immediately to mind. He had been a lawyer in Washington DC and is now living in Bolivia. He flies to Virginia twice a year to have his health work done and always makes a point to get in touch while in town and come and see me. If he has questions, he calls me from Bolivia; other times he e-mails me about problems or to get the information he needs. I find myself developing different relationships with people around issues that relate to managed care, pharmacy, and making things easier for our members."

fast facts

What do you need?
- Ability to perform research and analyze results
- Willingness to work closely with physicians, case managers, and other care givers
- Business and management skills
- Ability to interact with clients and solve their problems

What's it take?
- A current, active license to practice pharmacy
- Bachelor of Science (BS) or Doctor of Pharmacy (PharmD) degree*

Where will you practice?
- Health Maintenance Organizations
- Preferred Provider Organizations
- Care management programs

*Students graduating after Spring 2004 will be required to have a PharmD degree

military pharmacist

Military Pharmacist Checkpoint

Are you patriotic and disciplined?

Are you willing to travel?

Are you in shape and do you intend to stay that way?

If so, read on

A TRUE TALE

Commander Brian Kerr is an RPh, MS, MBA, and Medical Service Corps Officer in the United States Navy. During high school in Hull, Massachusetts, he worked nights and weekends at a hometown independent pharmacy. He

liked the idea that it was a gathering place in the neighborhood, and he admired the respect the proprietor commanded and the prosperity he seemed to enjoy.

Immediately after high school, Commander Kerr began his studies at Northeastern University's School of Pharmacy. But because of financial pressures, he had to drop out of school after only one year. He then enlisted in the Navy as a hospital corpsman, working in aviation medicine. Four years later in 1980, armed with financing from the GI bill, he returned to

pharmacy school. In 1984, Commander Kerr earned a Bachelor of Science degree in Pharmacy from the University of Rhode Island and quickly accepted a job at a chain drug store but soon after he realized being a chain druggist wasn't for him and he found himself thinking about returning to the service. "Even though the Navy initially paid less than an outside pharmacy position, its 30-day vacation policy, tax advantages and myriad opportunities made it look pretty good," he says. Once back in uniform, Commander Kerr returned to school aided by Navy-provided financing. In December 1988, he earned a Masters of Business Administration degree, awarded by the Rennselaer Polytechnic Institute. A decade later, he took another degree, a Masters of Science in Management from the Naval Postgraduate School in Monterey, California. "Not a lot of companies pay for your school and count the time spent there towards retirement," he says.

In his 20-year Naval career, Commander Kerr has had six tours of duty. Typically, a tour of duty lasts three years; Navy pharmacists generally have the option of remaining at their current duty station for a year or two beyond their original order; Commander Kerr explains that accepting a posting can be a negotiable process. During this 20-year period, Commander Kerr was posted at the Naval Hospital in Groton, Connecticut, and the Naval Air Station in Moffett Field, California. He served as a Division

Officer in the Pharmacy Department of the Naval Medical Center in Portsmouth Virginia, and the Department Head at the Naval Medical Clinic in Pearl Harbor, Hawaii, prior to attending Naval Postgraduate School. Then, in January 1999 he was named to head the Pharmacy Department of the Naval Hospital in Jacksonville, Florida, the post he currently holds. Except for a seven-month deployment during Operation Desert Storm, Commander Kerr has not been assigned overseas. However, the opportunity for international work is readily available.

Profiling the job

Of the more than 150 positions open to pharmacists in the United States Navy, approximately 20 percent can be vacant at any one time. This spells great opportunity for pharmacists hoping to work in this sector of the military.

Other opportunities for military pharmacists exist in the Army and Air Force (the Marines Corps use the Navy's pharmacies). In total, there are 561 authorized positions available in the uniformed services.

In addition to his primary duty of running the day-to-day operations of the pharmacy at the Naval Hospital in Jacksonville, Commander Kerr provides administrative oversight to seven Navy pharmacies along the eastern seaboard from Key West to Athens, Georgia. A staff of 70 pharmacists, including both military and civilian professional pharmacists, work at the Naval Hospital, which services approximately 100,000 active and retired members of the military and their eligible family members. It has a budget of $22 million. Handling patients from the 139-bed naval hospital is his main focus, but Commander Kerr's team actually fills many outpatient prescriptions as well. Outpatient prescription volume can reach 2,600 orders a day. In winter, when Florida attracts "snowbirds," the tally increases to 3,400, all of which are filled for free at no cost to patients eligible to use the military health system.

"While both civilian and military pharmacists make IVs and fill prescriptions, in the military you're handed more responsibility, you utilize technicians more than in the outside world and you always have that pack-your-bags phone call hanging over your head," says Commander Kerr. "You are a 24-hour-a-day representative of the USA. Your duty isn't done when your day shift ends," he says.

A day in the life

Commander Kerr usually arrives at the central pharmacy by 7:00am, a half-hour before it opens. Before the morning crew gathers to review charts and data from the previous day, he typically takes a moment to answer patient comments and to read and respond to email. Then he reviews his agenda. For example: What reports and evaluations are due? What budgets need approval? With what committees or pharmaceutical representatives is he slated to meet?

Commander Kerr often spends an hour or two of his day on the front lines filling prescriptions. The pharmacy at the Naval Hospital operates using what is called PODS, or Patient Orientated Dispensing System, where patients are served at up to 12 dispensing windows. When a patient steps up to the window, his or her medications are checked, filled, and patient counseling is provided. Up to 140 patients can be easily processed through the pharmacy in an hour.

Two of Commander Kerr's associate pharmacists round with physicians; Commander Kerr meets with his team of pharmacists as often as is necessary. Some of them serve on multi-disciplinary committees to either set up or improve the functioning of the different specialty clinics. Twice a year Commander Kerr visits each of the clinics that report to him. And recently, he's been meeting with patients to explain changes in their benefits. Specifically, eligible patients now have the choice of receiving their prescriptions by mail order or by visiting a local pharmacy affiliated with the Department of Defense, instead of just at military pharmacies.

"No matter how trivial a complaint or problem, it comes rolling back to my level. You've always got to have antenna out and be aware of what's going on in your department."

While civilian pharmacists could handle the retiree population, the nation's potential wartime needs virtually assure continued demand for military pharmacists, says Commander Kerr. Because of salary differences when compared to the private sector, the Navy as well as most Federal and State affiliated organizations have had increasing difficulty in attracting and retaining pharmacists. Now it's experimenting with "sweetening the pot" with innovative school tuition offers and an annual bonus.

"There are a lot of great things about being a pharmacist in the Service, not the least of which is the great travel opportunity due to the wide variety of postings and issues you deal with on each assignment. Certainly, you're never bored." After 20 years in the military, Commander Kerr is eligible for retirement at half his current pay and with generous benefits. Those benefits begin immediately upon retirement. And at a relatively young age of 44, he can work elsewhere if he so chooses.

PATIENT POINT OF VIEW

Commander Kerr recently attended meetings with Medicare eligible military retirees who no longer live on the base and their families. He explained the new regulations that allow these ex-servicemen to be provided with medications at a discount rate. "The Services have cut back on the free healthcare" said one World War II veteran. "But the pharmacy has always been there. This is a big step in restoring the benefits we've been promised."

fast facts

What do you need?
- ○ Ability to handle a lot of responsibility early in your career
- ○ Desire for foreign travel and frequent moves
- ○ Desire to work in and out of a hospital setting

What's it take?
- ○ A current, active license to practice pharmacy
- ○ Bachelor of Science (BS) or Doctor of Pharmacy (PharmD) degree*
- ○ Completion of a personal interview and satisfactory physical exam
- ○ U.S. citizenship

Where will you practice?
- ○ Army pharmacies
- ○ Navy pharmacies
- ○ Air Force pharmacies
- ○ Public Health Service pharmacies

*Students graduating after Spring 2004 will be required to have a PharmD degree

chapter fifteen
nuclear pharmacist

Nuclear Pharmacist Checkpoint

Can you focus and stay focused for long periods of time?

Are you prepared to have the same routine day after day?

Would you be comfortable handling radioactive materials?

If so, read on

A TRUE TALE

Walter Miller, PharmD, BCNP, had been an auto mechanic, radio station operator and insurance salesman before becoming a nuclear pharmacist. A nontraditional student who chose a nontraditional specialty, the 41-year-old

Dr. Miller is now national expansion manager for a leading supplier of radiopharmaceuticals. His company supplies time-sensitive medical products to hospitals and clinics.

Nuclear pharmacy involves the preparation of radioactive materials that will be used to diagnose specific diseases. These materials are generally injected into a patient's bloodstream or are swallowed, after which, gamma cameras scan the organs looking for the minute amounts of radioactive material. These scans provide the physician with a dynamic view of organ function. Other modalities, such as CT, MRI or X-ray, provide only structural information. It's a growing field, with more than 430 board certified nuclear pharmacists in the U.S.

Dr. Miller, who grew up in Lexington, Kentucky, attended Lindsey Wilson College in Columbia, Kentucky for pre-pharmacy and then proceeded to the University of Kentucky where he received his Bachelor of Science and PharmD degrees. Sorting career options at this top-ranked pharmaceutical school led him to pursue nuclear pharmacy. Dr. Miller joined his current company in Louisville, Kentucky in 1989 as an intern. While still on its staff, he spent two and a half years at a pharmacy in Charlotte, North Carolina before being transferred back full-time to Lexington to open, run and manage its operations.

Dr. Millner's company is the largest of a handful of organizations supplying the radiopharmaceuticals

> "Instead of dispensing 2000 to 3000 products, I deal only with 35 to 40, so I'm able to know each of them very well."

physicians use to gain their assessments. The Lexington store services 30 customers all in a radius of 2.5 hours from Lexington. On the other hand, the company's pharmacy in Franklin Square, New York has around 250 customers.

Profiling the job

In addition to preparing radiopharmaceutical agents, a nuclear pharmacist is responsible for quality control of these chemicals. Radiopharmaceuticals must meet certain USP compendium standards for purity, particle size and pH. While this generally is the responsibility of the drug manufacturers, it is up to the nuclear pharmacist to make sure the standards are upheld. Because of the radioactive nature of the materials, disposing of waste materials properly is an important responsibility within the pharmacist's realm. Uniform standards for this purpose have been set by the government and must be strictly adhered to in all institutions.

Meticulous record keeping matters, too. Nuclear pharmacists are responsible for reviewing patient charts prior to any testing. This procedure allows them to determine whether there are any other scheduled diagnostic tests for that time period which might use an incompatible agent. Sometimes medical conditions are present that might contraindicate the use of a radioactive drug, although, fewer than one in 300,000 patients develops an allergic reaction to radiopharmaceuticals.

Dr. Miller's team compounds the radiopharmaceuticals used in diagnostic imaging for 85 percent of the hospitals and clinics in Lexington. Most of the drugs are bound with the radioactive isotope technetium 99 M. But the other ingredients are determined by the organ function the physicians are monitoring. Some drugs offer high-resolution bone scans to help doctors look for fractures; others provide the best imaging for heart blockages. Sixty percent of the radiopharmaceuticals Dr. Miller prepares are for diagnostic cardiac studies.

Nuclear pharmacists earn about the same as those in retail and the job market is wide open. There are perhaps 4,000 nuclear pharmacists in the country and job openings for many more. That demand intensified when the training program went from three to four years leaving one year without any graduating pharmacists. Dr. Miller expects demand to remain strong.

Did you know?
After the Board of Pharmaceutical Specialties approved a petition in 1978, nuclear pharmacy became the world's first formally recognized pharmacy specialty practice.

A day in the life

The first of three pharmacists on staff opens the pharmacy at midnight. An hour later that pharmacist is joined by a pharmacy student and quality control lab technician. Together they ready 250 to 300 diagnostic compounds for morning delivery to hospitals in the area. Four drivers arrive at 1:00am, as well, to box the doses and prepare them for shipment by 4:00am. Another 50 or so prescriptions go out in the second run around 8:30am. Due to the short efficiency life of the nuclear chemicals, this process has to begin early. (Most of the products have a 12-hour life span although some expire within six hours.)

A second pharmacist arrives at 6:00am and replaces the midnight arrival. All pharmacists working with radioactive materials draw dosages, "in the hood," that is, behind a lead-lined laminar flow hood for protection and to assure sterility. Nuclear Regulatory Commission guidelines limit exposure to radioactivity and require pharmacists to be "safety-measured" frequently. Dr. Miller estimates that he, like most nuclear pharmacists, spends no more than four to five hours a day "in the hood." The rest of his eight-hour shift is spent handling documentation, printing prescriptions, wrapping syringes, re-stocking inventory and acting as clinical consultant. The third pharmacist arrives at 9:00am and the shifts rotate. A secretary handles the direct pay billing.

Dr. Miller doesn't mind getting up early but says that when he is on call it can be harried. In the six most recent days that Dr. Miller was on call, he had to return to the lab more than a dozen times to ready the needed products. In addition to readying the products, Dr. Miller teaches a nuclear medicine technology program and students rotate through his pharmacy for training. Each medical student spends 240 hours in the pharmacy. He also works with pharmacy students who do independent studies or rotations.

Dr. Miller loves his job, especially because it provides him with the opportunity to be an expert in all aspects of his field. He says the nuclear pharmacist's terrain is considerably more relaxed than that of a retail or hospital pharmacist. Although the general routine and intense focus required is the same every day, no day is ever the same. Calls from hospital and lab staff keep the day busy and varied. The variants in compounds keep him constantly doing tabulations in his head. Although many of the prescriptions are standing orders, each day a nuclear medicine technologist from each hospital calls to amend the order for the next day. "We rarely talk to the patient and we communicate with the radiologist only on a weekly basis," says Dr. Miller. "But I get great satisfaction from doing this and knowing it can save people's lives indirectly. I'm proud knowing I'm making a difference in someone's life."

fast facts

What do you need?
- Ability to serve as a Radiation Safety Officer (training is needed in areas such as radiation physics, biology and radiopharmaceutical chemistry, followed by one year of experience as a radiation safety technologist)
- Training in the handling of radioactive materials (can be obtained as part of PharmD or through company training)
- Ability to describe literature regarding radiopharmaceuticals to hospital and lab staff

What's it take?
- A current, active license to practice pharmacy
- Bachelor of Science (BS) or Doctor of Pharmacy (PharmD) degree*
- Designation as an "authorized user" of radioactive materials (issued by NRC or the state radiological division)
- One-year residency in nuclear pharmacy is preferred
- Board specialty in nuclear pharmacy is preferred

Where will you practice?
- Specialized pharmacies
- Imaging centers
- Hospitals
- Universities

*Students graduating after Spring 2004 will be required to have a PharmD degree

chapter sixteen
nutrition support pharmacist

**Nutrition
Support
Pharmacist
Checkpoint**

Are you
interested in
nutrition?

Are you
interested in
working on a
multidiscipli-
nary team?

Are you
interested in
metabolism,
biochemistry,
fluids and
electrolytes?

If so, read on

A TRUE TALE

Thirty years ago, at the age of six, Jeffrey Binkley, PharmD, developed Crohn's disease, a condition in which the bowel is chronically inflamed. The onset of this disease would eventually lead him into the career of a lifetime. Because of the nature of Crohn's, there were times, as Dr. Binkley was growing up, that he was unable to eat solid food. The alternative was to take his nourishment intravenously through a process known as total parenteral nutrition (TPN). TPN is an alternative means of feeding people who, for whatever reason, are unable to eat normally. The process involves insertion of a feeding tube into a vein and then attaching a bag of nutrients to that tube, which acts as a means of delivery. In his case, it was a pharmacist who mixed the formula and who administered it in his home. So Dr. Binkley's introduction to what a clinical pharmacist does was a uniquely personal one. "Before that, I thought pharmacists only stood behind a counter handing out pills. But here was a pharmacist managing my nutrition with a great deal of responsibility and respect from health professional peers," he says.

As a teenager, Dr. Binkley had thought he would eventually go to medical school. In keeping with his plan, he earned a bachelor's degree in chemistry from David Lipscomb University in Nashville in 1987. But for various reasons, Dr. Binkley decided to rethink the option of medical school. He still wanted to stay in the medical field. That's when he entered the University of Tennessee, College of Pharmacy in Memphis, where he eventually earned his PharmD degree in 1992. Dr. Binkley then moved on to the University of Maryland in Baltimore to complete a residency in nutrition support. That same year, he became a clinical pharmacist of nutrition

> "My work is especially gratifying for me because I've had a similar personal experience. I have been in the shoes of my patients and have a great respect for what they're going through."

support at Vanderbilt University. As good luck would have it, the pharmacist who introduced him to nutrition support, and who tended to him as a youth, eventually became his mentor. He ultimately succeeded her at the job she'd had for 10 years, when she left to become a full-time mother.

Profiling the job

As a nutrition support pharmacist, Dr. Binkley, who became board certified in 1995, is responsible for all of the hospital's TPN patients. He makes sure the therapy they are receiving is complete and specific to their needs. In doing this, Dr. Binkley factors in the patient's whole medical history, current condition and concurrent disease states before devising a nutrition formula that will provide the necessary fluids, carbohydrates, fats, proteins, electrolytes, vitamins and trace elements. The patient's age, organ function and disease processes are among the parameters that affect his plan. Dr. Binkley is also charged with seeing that the administration of the TPN is done properly. At Vanderbilt, this can mean he sees up to 25 patients a day. His patients include people who are unable to eat normally as a result of bowel surgery, short bowel syndrome, Crohn's disease, colitis, pancreatitis, and failure of certain organs specific to digestion.

Approximately 60 percent of Dr. Binkley's in-hospital patients have a formula change daily. Generally a 24-hour infusion is prescribed, but he can write the formula to provide the same amount of total energy delivered over a shorter time. For most patients the duration of TPN therapy is relatively short, but some are maintained on it for life.

In addition to the parenteral arena, the nutrition support pharmacist must be well grounded in enteral feeding formulations and in co-administration of medications. He must be expert in the composition and compatibility of nutrients and the interaction between drugs and nutrients. Although some of the members of the pharmacy staff compound the nutrition regimen he formulates, Dr. Binkley is responsible for making sure the actual formula can be safely dispensed and administered, depending upon its stability and compatibility with other medications that the patient is taking. Any incorrect balance can cause complications. One frequently encountered complication is the effects of overfeeding. Most patients tolerate their therapy well if adequately managed, but hyperglycemia, liver problems and respiratory problems are possible. "A lot of times folks think that more is better," says Dr. Binkley. "Over-nutrition is one of the problems we run up against."

Did you know?
Nutrition support pharmacy was recognized as a specialty in 1988.

A day in the life

Dr. Binkley usually arrives at the Hospital's central pharmacy by 8:00am to review the list of TPN patients. He then makes rounds to evaluate each one. Throughout the day, Dr. Binkley consults with other pharmacists, dietitians, physicians, nurses, nurse practitioners and social workers about the nutritional regimen he designs — or changes he proposes — "so that everybody is on the same page." Then they all make rounds as a team at 2:00pm.

In addition to devising patient regimens, Dr. Binkley spends his time preparing for lectures that he must deliver as part of his job. The audiences for these include nursing and pharmacy students, practicing pharmacists and hospital house staff. He is also responsible for evaluating new products and for sharing what he's learned with all team members and their patients.

One downside to work in this area, Dr. Binkley laments, is the reluctance of many hospitals to treat nutrition as a separate entity, especially in the current climate of major downsizing. In fact, his own team dynamics have changed three times in the seven years he has been here. "Larger hospitals tend to have a team and smaller ones tend to rely on the staff pharmacist," he says. Even so, Dr. Binkley feels that if he had the chance to do it over again, he'd stay the course. "It's rewarding, interesting and very satisfying. I wouldn't wish Crohn's on anyone, but I'm grateful that it led me to something I love."

PATIENT POINT OF VIEW

Since 1993, Dr. Binkley has known a 42-year-old woman suffering from short bowel syndrome, who had been on home TPN for the past 20 years. Her once active life has been increasingly circumscribed. In each of the three to four times a year she's been admitted to the hospital, Dr. Binkley has attended her; they have become friends. He also maintains a close relationship with her mother, son and sister, and he regularly calls to see how she's doing. Whenever a visiting nurse broaches the subject of nutrition she insists on calling Dr. Binkley. "I won't let anyone else see me," she says. "If he isn't around, I tell them to page him until they find him!"

fast facts

What do you need?
○ Ability to work well with patients
○ Ability to function as a member of a multidisciplinary team
○ Creativity in designing treatments specific to a patient's needs

What's it take?
○ A current, active license to practice pharmacy
○ Bachelor of Science (BS) or Doctor of Pharmacy (PharmD) degree*
○ Board certification in Nutrition Support Pharmacy is preferred

Where will you practice?
○ Acute and subacute care facilities
○ Ambulatory clinics
○ Skilled nursing facilities
○ Patients' homes

*Students graduating after Spring 2004 will be required to have a PharmD degree

oncology pharmacist

**Oncology
Pharmacist
Checkpoint**

Are you
compassionate?

Are you
sympathetic,
yet tough
enough to see
pain and
suffering with-
out being
emotionally
drawn into it?

Are you
self-motivated
enough to con-
tinue to learn
in a rapidly
changing field?

If so, read on

A TRUE TALE

Alicia Kniska, BS, PharmD, BCOP, is the sole pharmacist working within
the University of Maryland Medical System's bone marrow transplant
program. Dr. Kniska grew up loving the field of medicine in general but
couldn't reconcile herself to some of the requirements for becoming a physician. She discovered pharmacy through a favorite uncle who owned his own
drug store in Bridgeport, West Virginia. For her, pharmacy encompassed the

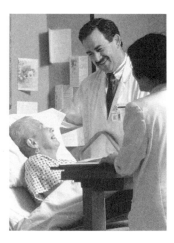

best parts of medicine — interacting with
people and helping them. So when it came
time for her to make a career choice, she
opted for pharmacy. And when it came
time to specialize as a pharmacist, she
gravitated to oncology. Why did she choose
it? "I had lost relatives and friends to cancer,
and I hoped in my own way that I could
be part of a team that works with these
very sick people, and still stay involved
with pharmacy."

After earning a Bachelor of Science degree
in pharmacy at West Virginia University,
Dr. Kniska worked for a year as a staff
pharmacist specializing in chemotherapy at
the West Virginia University Hospital. Her community practice experiences
during rotations exposed her to various subspecialties and she quickly
learned what she wanted — or in her case, what she didn't want: one facility
was too busy for the pharmacist to adequately connect patients and another
was too slowly paced. This is when she realized that by entering the subspe-
cialty of clinical oncology, she would be put in direct contact with cancer
patients in a medical setting, while still practicing pharmacy.

After a residency in oncology pharmacy, Dr. Kniska earned a PharmD
degree, spent a year at the Anderson Cancer Center in Houston and then
moved on to the University of Kentucky, where she further defined her
training to include a focus on clinical stem cell transplantation. In 1996,
when the University of Maryland Medical System in Baltimore opened a
bone marrow transplant program, Dr. Kniska was ready for the job.

Profiling the job

Like most oncology pharmacists, Dr. Kniska reviews drug orders. Her responsibility is to ensure that the orders are accurate and complete, and in keeping with the patient's laboratory results. When compounding drugs, pharmacists at the University of Maryland mix their chemotherapy drugs in a bacteria-free area designed to create a sterile, protective environment. Special gowns and gloves are worn by all workers coming in contact with the chemicals, to protect both themselves and the medicine. This is part of Dr. Kniska's job in addition to making the daily rounds of the transplant patients with the oncology team. Her daily routine also includes tracking drug and toxicity levels, teaching nurses and other members of the team and reviewing new study protocols.

Facilitating research studies is another aspect of her work. When a patient agrees to participate in an oncologic clinical trial, Dr. Kniska plays a large role. She must make sure that each of the patients enrolled receives the accurate dose of the drug at the specific time as dictated in the protocol. This is not a task to be taken lightly — each aspect of the data collected must be "clean," or error free.

In addition to the 15 lectures a year she delivers, Dr. Kniska participates on clinical review committees, providing information on a drug's availability, dosing suggestions, interactions and monitoring techniques. She often requests that certain new drugs be added to the unit's formulary. Drug usage evaluations are also important. Because cancer patients are generally on more than one medication — typically chemotherapy and anti-nausea drugs, for example — she determines which drugs can safely be given together.

"When I see a patient who has been in the hospital for a month recover and go home, I'm on top of the world. When they come into the clinic for a checkup and they're still fine, I can't think of a better reward for those of us who have helped them get there," she says.

There are other benefits to the job as well. As a specialist, Dr. Kniska speculates that she earns a 10 percent premium over other hospital pharmacists, and has the advantage of regular hours as well. "Being part of a team has its benefits," she says. "I learn something new every day from at least one of my colleagues. The nurses, nurse practitioners, physician assistants and attending physicians with whom I round, personify medicine at its finest. It's great to be part of a team that takes such high-quality care of patients," she says.

Did you know? Board certification for oncology pharmacists went into effect in 1996. There are at least 1,000 oncology pharmacists in the U.S. now. In 2000, 118 passed the exam.

A day in the life

The first thing Dr. Kniska does when she arrives at work is review the patient census for the 16 beds in the transplant unit. She then examines the patients' charts and lab results as well as additions to the drug therapy profiles that were written in her absence. Dr. Kniska ascertains that everything prescribed has been appropriately dosed, and then rounds with physicians and nurses. On rounds, she checks patients' IV fluids to make sure the bags are dispensing the prescribed drugs correctly and monitors the patients for drug interactions and adverse reactions. Each patient's regime is totally individualized. On average ten patients a day will require medication changes.

"No one can predict with 100 percent accuracy how any patient will respond to their therapies. All we know are the percentages," she says.

"There's no such thing as a standard dose of chemotherapy, but there is a standard question. Almost every cancer sufferer wants to know what he or she should do, what treatment they should take"

Dr. Kniska tries to "stay away from the numbers game," leaving the physicians to discuss probability outcomes. Instead, she concentrates on giving specific non-biased information on the investigative trials going on.

PATIENT POINT OF VIEW

The 35-year old woman diagnosed with ovarian cancer initially had responded well to the chemotherapy, but then relapsed. For some reason, Dr. Kniska felt an emotional connection with this patient. When she saw her in clinic, she informed the woman about the chemotherapy process and discussed both current treatments and ongoing clinical trials that were enrolling. Dr. Kniska tries not to influence a patient's choice of treatment, although the woman — like many patients — wanted to know what Dr. Kniska would do if the chance to participate in a clinical trial were offered to her. "I explain that most often there isn't any one treatment or drug that's clearly better than the other. If there was one that was far better than another," she explained, "we would use the better one. No question." Each cancer is different and each person is different and that all comes into play.

fast facts

What do you need?
- Board certification as an oncology pharmacist
- Caution and sensitivity to work in an arena where experimental drug therapies are frequently used
- Ability to recognize the balance between improved survival and quality of life

What's it take?
- A current, active license to practice pharmacy
- Bachelor of Science (BS) or Doctor of Pharmacy (PharmD) degree*
- One-year residency may be required
- Board certification in oncology pharmacy is preferred
- Hospital pharmacy experience, preferably in a critical care setting

Where will you practice?
- Hospitals
- Universities
- Cancer centers

*Students graduating after Spring 2004 will be required to have a PharmD degree

chapter eighteen
operating room pharmacist

Operating Room Pharmacist Checkpoint

Do you generally develop good collegial relationships and communicate well?

Can you handle stress and prioritize effectively?

Do you have good drug information retrieval skills?

If so, read on

A TRUE TALE

Andrew Donnelly, PharmD must have had a pretty influential cousin because both he and his twin brother became pharmacists, just as their

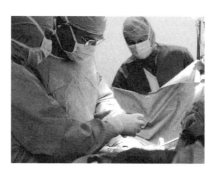

cousin had about 15 years earlier. During high school his cousin convinced him that pharmacy offered an opportunity to combine science with medicine, patient care, and business. He applied to pharmacy school and has never regretted his decision. Today, with PharmD and MBA degrees to his credit, Dr. Donnelly is an Assistant Director of Pharmacy at Rush-Presbyterian-St. Luke's Medical Center in Chicago, where he also serves as a clinical pharmacist in the Operating Room and Anesthesiology department.

Dr. Donnelly received his Doctor of Pharmacy degree from the University of Illinois College of Pharmacy, while working part-time in the University's hospital pharmacy. In 1989, after nine years at the Hospital — during which time he established and supervised its OR pharmacy — he left to pursue an opportunity at Rush-Presbyterian-St. Luke's Medical Center.

Originally, Dr. Donnelly intended to become a retail pharmacist, but those aspirations got side-tracked when he realized that practicing in a hospital would allow him to use the skills he enjoyed most. He knew he had found a home when he started working in the operating room.

At Rush, the 43-year-old Donnelly wears many academic and administrative hats. He has faculty appointments at the Chicago College of Pharmacy, the University of Illinois College of

"Every day in the OR brings a new group of patients with a new set of problems. There is certainly no set routine in terms of workflow. Things can be intensely quiet one minute and move at the speed of light the next. A patient can go from being fine to 'crashing' within seconds. You've got to be able to respond quickly to whatever situation arises."

Pharmacy, and the College of Health Sciences at Rush University. He is also the pharmacy department's residency director and is responsible for coordinating the clinical services provided by the pharmacist staff at Rush. Yet with all this on his agenda, he is still able to devote a significant amount of his time to his work within the hospital's operating room. As an OR practitioner, Dr. Donnelly feels that he has much to offer. "The OR pharmacist is truly a valued member of the healthcare team. My opinion makes a difference and I know my contributions positively impact patient care. I would pick OR pharmacy practice again in a heartbeat."

Profiling the job

An average of 85 surgeries are performed daily in the 27 operating suites at Rush. The majority of these are elective procedures, but transplant or other emergency surgery can be done with little advance notice. Most surgeries require an array of drugs specific to that particular operation. As an OR pharmacist, Dr. Donnelly is responsible for seeing that the appropriate medications are available and ready for the surgery being performed. He oversees a diverse pharmacopoeia of drugs. Medications routinely used by anesthesia providers include opioids for intraoperative analgesia; induction agents to make the patient unconscious; neuromuscular blocking agents to facilitate intubation and maintain muscle relaxation during surgery; benzodiazepines to reduce anxiety and produce sedation in the patient prior to surgery; antiemetics for the prevention or treatment of postoperative nausea and vomiting; antiarrhythmic agents to control irregular heart rhythms; colloids to counter the effects of blood loss; vasopressors to increase blood pressure; and vasodilators to decrease blood pressure. Medications typically used by surgeons are, in general, less complex and fewer in number when compared to anesthesia providers and include local anesthetics, topical hemostats to control bleeding, antibiotic irrigations for use in the surgical incision, contrast media for x-rays, and antibiotic infusions to prevent postoperative infection.

Operating room pharmacy practice has progressed tremendously since the early years when the pharmacist was mainly responsible for medication preparation and distribution. Today OR pharmacists must factor economics into their daily practice, the reality of every healthcare professional working in a hospital. The modern day OR is no longer always considered a profit center but rather, in many cases, a cost center. In general, a hospital receives a set reimbursement from the "payer" — the insurance company — for a

Did you know?
In a 1990 survey performed by the Operating Room Pharmacy Services Association, there were 162 functioning OR pharmacies in the U.S. Today, this number is thought to be at least double that reported in 1990.

surgical procedure. The amount is predetermined by the payer based on cost evaluations of prior identical surgeries. As such, a major role of the OR pharmacist is to ensure rational, cost-effective drug therapy is used.

Operating Room pharmacists, especially those working in major medical centers, are educators as well. They serve as drug information resources in the OR. They keep a diverse library of reference books in the pharmacy and use the Internet as an information source routinely. Dr. Donnelly becomes involved in the medication-related research occurring in the OR, and has served as co-investigator on several clinical studies. He also is involved in teaching pharmacy students, and has developed an OR rotation for students interested in this area; additionally, he teaches nurse anesthetist and perfusion students.

But Dr. Donnelly is not only a teacher. He, like all pharmacists, is a student, too. When initially entering this practice setting, Dr. Donnelly was confronted with a group of drugs that receive little attention in most pharmacy school curriculums. As a result, he had to do a significant amount of learning on his own to understand how these drugs work, how they are used in conjunction with other drugs given in the operating room, their potential for drug interactions, and their side effect profile. Since new drugs are constantly being approved and released, including ones for use during surgery, Dr. Donnelly spends a significant amount of time reading medical and pharmacy journals and attending national meetings to keep current.

Dr. Donnelly cites advantages to his area of practice perhaps not so readily seen in other practice settings. Since there are a relatively limited number of OR pharmacists, he remarks, there is a greater opportunity to be invited to speak on OR-related topics at national professional meetings. Opportunities also abound to publish in this area, to serve on editorial boards of anesthesia-related publications, to sit on advisory committees and to consult on OR pharmacy services. There is, however, little opportunity for direct patient contact in this setting when compared to more traditional settings in which pharmacists practice.

A day in the life

On days he is scheduled to work in the OR pharmacy, Dr. Donnelly arrives at the hospital at either 6:00am for the early shift, or 10:00am for the late, rotating shifts with the other OR pharmacists. Two pharmacy technicians round out the pharmacy staff and work the same shifts as the pharmacists.

Dr. Donnelly prefers the early shift as the first surgeries of the day begin at approximately 7:00am. "This is the time the majority of questions, issues, and problems will arise. By physically being present in the OR area, we encourage questions, and get them, dozens a day."

After a 6:00am arrival, Dr. Donnelly scans the OR schedule, reviewing the types of procedures planned for the day and identifying solutions and medications needed for the surgical cases. He looks for any patient-specific information that would influence medication preparation.

It is standard practice for the OR nurses to call the surgeons' medication requests to the OR pharmacy in advance. This allows him to prepare the medications and compound the intravenous solutions so they are ready to go when the nurse arrives at the pharmacy prior to the start of surgery.

"For the most part, surgeons know exactly what they will need for their procedures," Dr. Donnelly says. However, when a patient is on the table and the surgeon needs an unexpected medication prepared, they advise him through an intercom and Dr. Donnelly or his colleagues ready it quickly.

Dr. Donnelly and his colleagues spend about two hours daily tracking the controlled substances used by the anesthesia providers and surgeons. As part of the controlled substance system in place at Rush, returned syringes are randomly tested to ensure that the content of the syringe is just what is stated on the label. A pharmacy's willingness to assume responsibility for controlled substance dispensing and record keeping has been used to help justify the establishment of a pharmacy within the OR.

"Working in the OR pharmacy is highly unpredictable — you never know when a case is going to go bad or when you are going to get medication requests or questions from numerous OR suites all at once. You've got to be ready to respond. Being able to effectively prioritize the requests is critical."

To round out the day, Dr. Donnelly might attend a meeting with other members of the healthcare team to develop drug use guidelines or update treatment protocols for surgery patients. To prepare for these meetings Dr. Donnelly will have done his "homework," which could mean studying patients' operating room records

"In the early days, OR pharmacies were established because controlled substance accountability in the operating rooms of many institutions was less than optimal. This was often reflected in the findings of the various regulatory groups responsible for accrediting the hospital."

Andrew Donnelly, PharmD, MBA

for drug use patterns or evaluating the literature to determine what is being done at other institutions.

PATIENT POINT OF VIEW

A surgeon calls the OR pharmacy and requests an antibiotic for his patient. Dr. Donnelly asks if the patient has any allergies and is told that the patient is allergic to penicillin. Dr. Donnelly informs the surgeon that there is cross-sensitivity between the antibiotic ordered and penicillin so there is a possibility that the patient is also allergic to the requested antibiotic. He gives the surgeon several recommendations of appropriate antibiotics to use. Although the patient will never know that this exchange took place and that a potentially serious situation has been avoided, Dr. Donnelly sees one of his major roles as being a "watchdog" for the patient when it comes to medication use in the OR.

>>> fast facts

What do you need?
- Ability to deal with emergency situations
- Thorough knowledge of anesthesia and surgery medications
- Basic understanding of the anesthesia machine and monitors
- Ability to function as part of a multidisciplinary team
- Willingness to learn on own

What's it take?
- A current, active license to practice pharmacy
- Bachelor of Science (BS) or Doctor of Pharmacy (PharmD) degree*
- Hospital pharmacy experience, preferably in a critical care setting

Where will you practice?
- Hospitals (operating room pharmacy satellites)
- Ambulatory surgicenters

*Students graduating after Spring 2004 will be required to have a PharmD degree

pediatric pharmacist

A TRUE TALE

"Many pharmacists shy away from pediatrics, not just because drug dosing and delivery is more complicated than it is with adults, but because of the emotional issues of dealing with sick children," says 46-year-old pediatric pharmacist Robert Kuhn, PharmD. But pediatric pharmacy has its rewards too, he adds. It offers benefits both in the interesting variety of the patients' conditions and in the emotional rewards attendant on making an ill child well again. "Our patients run the spectrum in age [newborns to seventeen or so], and weight [850-gram newborns to 200-pound teens]. They present every condition and disease state from trauma to transplant. Just figuring out what will work becomes more intricate because you have to factor in so many different components — things like age, weight and severity of condition affect every decision. Dosing is far more complicated too, as so much of it is specific to the child. Delivering two milligrams of an antibiotic to a tiny newborn is pretty challenging," says Dr. Kuhn. "You've really got to focus on the details. One small mistake can be catastrophic to kids, especially to premature babies. With an 800-gram baby, things can go bad fast." On the other hand, if the right problem is diagnosed and the right treatment prescribed, children tend to mend faster.

"Kids are like mirrors, reflecting how they feel. I have a theory, which I call 'The positive hallway sign.' If a kid is running up and down the hall or asking for Playstation®, it's a better indication they're on the mend than some of the scientific tests. Saying they can go home and watching the smiles light up their faces is always a bonus for the entire staff."

Before becoming a pharmacist, Dr. Kuhn earned an undergraduate degree in philosophy from the Franciscan University of Steubenville, in Ohio, in 1976. One summer during his college years, he shadowed a pharmacist. "He did everything from changing watch batteries to recommending therapeutic agents," says Dr. Kuhn admiringly. "There

Pediatric Pharmacist Checkpoint

Can you overcome the fear of working with a sick child?

Would you feel comfortable with the plethora of delivery approaches and dosing that pediatrics require?

Would you welcome the variety and constant newness each situation poses?

If so, read on

was no end to the number of different things he took on in a day." With that role model in mind, he pursued, and received, a Bachelor of Science degree in pharmacy from Ohio State in 1980. For the next 18 months, he worked as a clinical pharmacist in the Toledo Hospital, an 800-bed facility, preparing IVs, rounding with physicians and dispensing medications. A two-year stint afterward at the University of Texas led to a Doctor of Pharmacy degree. After completing a fellowship in pediatric pharmacy in 1985, Dr. Kuhn joined the University of Kentucky where he is currently a professor in the Pharmacy Practice and Science Division of the University of Kentucky College of Pharmacy and Vice Chair of Ambulatory Care.

Did you know?
More than 200 million prescriptions are written annually for children and teenagers.

Profiling the job

Pediatric pharmacists practice in a variety of settings from academia to children's hospitals, from large medical centers to smaller community hospitals. The setting influences, if not determines, their ancillary duties. In Dr. Kuhn's case, working at a university hospital requires administrative duties, including committee work on drug policy, editing the *Kentucky Society of Hospital Pharmacists* newsletter, and lecturing before students, nurses, and physicians at least once a week. No matter where he or she practices, though, a successful pediatric pharmacist must be able to integrate general pharmaceutical information with that specific to pediatric drug therapy. And they should be available as needed. Often, this will include a visit to distraught parents in their time of need. Indeed, that's the worst thing about pediatric pharmacy, Dr. Kuhn concedes, "the terribly sick children." He consoles himself knowing that what he does makes a difference, far more often than not. "Our medications can help a child live longer or at least have an improved quality of life," he says.

A day in the life

Dr. Kuhn specializes in respiratory diseases, particularly cystic fibrosis, of which there are some 30,000 sufferers in the U.S. He gravitated towards this arena after attending his first cystic fibrosis camp in 1978. While there's no such thing as a "typical day" for him, Dr. Kuhn says, in a "typical" week he sees between 35 and 40 patients in his clinic, and consults with perhaps 30 parents. He also regularly rounds with physicians and pharmacy students, administers drugs in the clinic and hospital, and consults closely with house staff and attending physicians on patient treatment. At least 10 hours a week are devoted to research in his field of pulmonary medicine, especially research concerning cystic fibrosis, drug delivery and xenobiotic transfer. In the past 15 years he has trained 18 pediatric pharmacy residents.

Dr. Kuhn says his job has taught him to value his own "pediatric population" at home — his two young sons. Although he works on average 55 to 60 hours a week, he tries to leave the university every day in time to eat dinner with his family. Still, he regularly receives weekend calls asking for his advice and recommendations for therapies and alternatives. "I'm consulted on the tough cases. Everyone knows how to dose amoxicillin but the proper use of sodium arginine is a different story," he says.

"I used to think that pharmacists were the folks who only helped you with medications, but in 20 years I've seen it's a portal to diversity. You can be a clinical specialist in a hospital, in research, in corporate life, anywhere. It's a wide-open field."

Pediatric pharmacy is a cottage industry that's booming because of a dramatic shortage of qualified candidates. His current resident is being recruited by several children's hospitals around the country with an average annual salary of $70,000. When you figure in outside consulting and lecturing, a pediatric pharmacist could earn $125,000, he says.

But Dr. Kuhn says his compensation is markedly boosted by the gift of being in contact with the special children and families whose experience he shares. "If that doesn't change you, something's not right," he says. Dr. Kuhn himself was changed when his youngest son was born prematurely and spent 15 days in a neonatal intensive care unit. "While the experience was a harrowing one, it has allowed me to talk, firsthand, to parents about their fears and issues and to know more accurately how they feel."

Being around sick children has reinforced Dr. Kuhn's belief in the possibility of miracles. Recently, a two-year-old girl had a cardiac arrest during a diagnostic procedure, and the medical team frantically used the defibrillator paddles to establish a heart rhythm. No one was optimistic that she would survive, much less survive with a normal quality of life. But amazingly, three days after that incident, she awoke from a coma, ate scrambled eggs and walked out of the hospital, fit and healthy.

PATIENT POINT OF VIEW

The girl, suffering from cystic fibrosis, was almost 16 and had been to the hospital more than 15 times in the past seven years. Dr. Kuhn had watched her suffer for a long time. She was in the final stages of the fatal disease and not responding well to medicine. He sorrowfully told her mother that they had taken drug therapy and medical management as far as it could go — that he'd make certain she was comfortable on morphine or valium, but that there was not a whole lot more he could offer them. The mother understood, he says, and she was grateful for the extra time the care provided for her daughter. "You have offered us so much already," the woman told him, "You have helped my daughter and me more than I can say."

>>> fast facts

What do you need?
- o Desire to work with children
- o Strong oral and written communications skills
- o Strong investigative, research, and problem-solving skills

What's it take?
- o A current, active license to practice pharmacy
- o Bachelor of Science (BS) or Doctor of Pharmacy (PharmD) degree*
- o One-year general residency followed by a specialty residency in pediatric pharmacy may be required

Where will you practice?
- o Children's hospitals
- o Hospitals
- o Universities
- o Cancer centers

*Students graduating after Spring 2004 will be required to have a PharmD degree

chapter twenty
the pharmacist in a grocery chain

A TRUE TALE

As manager of clinical pharmacy services for the Dominick's Finer Foods supermarket chain, Judy Sommers Hanson, PharmD, helps her store's pharmacists develop and execute community programs that make health care more accessible to her patients. The 31-year-old native of Chicago says,

"Being a supermarket pharmacist today encompasses far more than the usual counting, measuring, pouring, packaging, labeling and compounding drugs." Today, she continues, it includes the role of drug-use counselor, public relations practitioner and enterprising pioneer. Now supermarket pharmacists experiment with new programs that help more people take control of their own health care. Many supermarkets are remodeling their pharmacies and even adding private consultation rooms to accommodate the new functions they have begun to offer.

In 1991, Dr. Sommers Hanson earned a Bachelors of Science in chemistry from DePaul University in Chicago and went directly to the University of Illinois at Chicago College of Pharmacy, where she earned her Doctorate of Pharmacy four years later. In 1995, she undertook an unusual community pharmacy residency sponsored by both the St. Louis College of Pharmacy and a chain of independent pharmacies. At the time, there were only 10 community pharmacy residencies across the country. Dr. Sommers Hanson worked with her preceptor to make suggestions about the remodeling of the store, what types of services to implement and the marketing plan. She also worked with patients to ensure their drug therapies were meeting its intended goals. This, she says, was rather advanced for community pharmacy practice at the time.

A year later Dr. Sommers Hanson applied to Dominick's grocery chain to develop a pharmacy care program in collaboration with the University of Illinois at Chicago College of Pharmacy. At that time Dominick's had 87 pharmacies; now there are 105. Currently, 20 stores in the chain offer pharmacist's clinical interaction with patients. In addition to her work at Dominick's, Dr. Sommers Hanson is currently Adjunct Clinical Faculty with

The Pharmacist in a Grocery Chain Checkpoint

Do you want to put your clinical training to the test?

Would the array of programming opportunities that practicing in a non-traditional setting interest you?

Would long hours suit you?

If so, read on

the University of Illinois. This is a volunteer position given to preceptors of University of Illinois at Chicago College of Pharmacy students. "In this role I precept students during clerkship rotations at the pharmacy, serve as a guest lecturer on community pharmacy practice topics, and as the primary preceptor for the Community Pharmacy Practice residency."

Profiling the job

Supermarkets are the fastest growing outlet for prescription drugs, accounting for 12 percent of unit sales and 11 percent of dollar sales in 1999. While overall prescription sales climbed nine percent, supermarket sales almost doubled that, surging 17 percent. At Dominick's, Dr. Sommers Hanson and her team have developed several pharmacy programs with the goal of implementation across the entire Dominick's supermarket chain. She currently provides these services out of her home store in Buffalo Grove, Illinois. However, she also provides health screening programs for cholesterol and diabetes throughout the chain. Dr. Sommers Hanson has also gone to the other pharmacy sites to provide consultations at the request of a patient or pharmacist.

Not all supermarket pharmacists do what Dr. Sommers Hanson does. Others might be involved with selling and servicing durable medical equipment, sickroom supplies, respiratory and physical therapy products, diagnostic and testing products and ostomy supplies. Forty-nine percent of supermarkets now offer a disease management program in at least one in store pharmacy, according to the Food Marketing Institute (FMI). The top issues are typically diabetes, hyperlipidemia, asthma, hypertension and smoking cessation. The FMI found that 90 percent of the supermarket pharmacists it surveyed offer blood pressure testing and 86 percent offer flu shots. More than half, offer in-store cholesterol testing, blood glucose monitoring and wellness tours.

Financially, Dominick's has not yet broken even on the project, Dr. Sommers Hanson admits. Management expects it to take another two years before the program is profitable. But those numbers don't reflect the volume of customers who have been attracted or retained because of the service. Then too, the pharmacy care program is a defensive move. Other chains have established programs like this. "I'd be hard pressed to say it's on every corner but everyone is trying something," says Dr. Sommers Hanson.

A major hurdle the program faces is convincing insurance companies that what the pharmacists do is effective and worthy of coverage. "They want data to prove it," says Dr. Sommers Hanson. Physician relations is another important part of her job. "Physicians are pulled in so many different directions and they are ultimately responsible for the patient's care," she says. "We try hard to keep them informed." If they detect a problem in one of the clinics, the pharmacy recommends changes, but it's up to the physician to endorse them.

A day in the life

In addition to her role as clinical practitioner, Dr. Sommers Hanson also works with the University of Illinois faculty to train students for this role. She develops programs with pharmaceutical companies, visits other pharmacies in the Dominick's chain to evaluate work flow patterns, reviews pharmacists' techniques on things like blood glucose monitoring, and recommends changes that will in effect free the pharmacists' time behind the counter and make more time for direct patient counseling.

Dr. Sommers Hanson spends about half of her time in the store and the remainder of that time managing program development for the pharmacy. "When I started with Dominick's, my main focus was working in the store with patients. Now, I do a lot less of that and more of developing programs and models to optimize performance of all the pharmacies within the Dominick's chain." This can take her to various sites throughout the chain, her division headquarters or to the University of Illinois. In the scope of her week, at least two days are devoted to on-the-counter work, which entails a lot of working with patients to provide counseling services. It would not be uncommon for Dr. Sommers Hanson to be verifying prescriptions, then sitting down with a patient to counsel him or her about taking their blood pressure and addressing their medication concerns.

"For a women's health program we're focusing on cooking with soy and women's supplements and working with people from the marketing, community affairs and pharmacy departments. Because we are in supermarket, I like to pick things available to our store customers, such as our soy products, calcium fortified cereals, and orange juice."

She finds her work exciting and fresh. "I learn something new every day," she says. But she concedes that the days can be long. Dr. Sommers Hanson often puts in 12 to 14 hours before going home. Dr. Sommers Hanson eventually sees herself moving more into a corporate position, helping others operate at peak capacity and persuading them of the best way to run their practice.

Implementing patient care programs throughout the chain will take more time than originally expected, Dr. Sommers Hanson says. "After all it took a decade to entrench similar programs in hospitals. But we need to change the way we do business and this is the greatest thing." she says.

PATIENT POINT OF VIEW

For two years, the 72-year-old diabetes patient had come around to give Dr. Sommers Hanson a weekly update on his condition. Lately he'd been dropping by with donuts for "his Judy." Before Dr. Sommers Hanson reviewed his condition with him, he had not been aware that his high blood sugar was related to food intake. He hadn't spent time with his physician. "By putting the pieces together you've told me more about my diabetes than anyone else," he recently told her, grateful for her kind attentiveness. "If you weren't seeing me I doubt I'd be in control."

>>> **fast facts**

What do you need?
- Strong customer service skills
- Ability to communicate effectively
- Business and management skills

What's it take?
- A current, active license to practice pharmacy
- Bachelor of Science (BS) or Doctor of Pharmacy (PharmD) degree*

Where will you practice?
- Supermarkets
- Corporate headquarters

*Students graduating after Spring 2004 will be required to have a PharmD degree

pharmacists in non-traditional settings

THE SKY'S THE LIMIT

These days, for every pharmacist behind a counter there are an equal number who are working in other venues. Combining pharmacy and law, for instance, is one intellectually satisfying and rewarding career. For today's pharmacist seeking a dual career — or something just a little bit imaginative — the door is wide open and the sky's the limit.

The Pharmacist Attorney

Edward D. Rickert, Esq., who holds degrees in both pharmacy and law, is a perfect example of someone who has successfully integrated a dual career. Rickert received his BS in pharmacy from the University of Iowa School of Pharmacy in 1983. As an undergraduate, he took a class called Pharmacy

Law which, he says, provided him with the inspiration to go to law school. "Pharmacy law is totally different from anything else you learn in pharmacy school," Rickert says. "In general, pharmacy is strictly science-based — there are specific right and wrong answers. It's black and white, and you have to memorize a good deal. Law, on the other hand, is more amorphous. There often is no right or wrong answer, and you need to figure out what could happen under a particular set of circumstances. You analyze and weigh many factors, and decide on a course of action. Rather than dealing with black and white, there is a lot of 'gray area' in law. Many pharmacy students are too scientifically oriented to enjoy that part, but I found it extremely appealing and still do."

After graduating from pharmacy school, Rickert worked in a hospital pharmacy for two years before applying and being accepted to the Chicago Kent School of Law. He continued to work in retail pharmacy throughout law school, despite being a full-time student.

"My pharmacy degree has been tremendously helpful in private law practice," Rickert says. "The way the legal market is nowadays, it helps to have a specialty that sets you apart from all the other attorneys out there." Today, from 60 to 70 percent of what Rickert does is pharmacy related, with much of his work in litigation. Rickert currently works with a number of chain and independent pharmacies where he represents the pharmacy or individual pharmacists who, for various reasons, are called before their state pharmacy boards. He also handles the legal issues for mail order pharmacy providers and pharmacy benefit management companies. One of Rickert's clients is an insurance company that insures both pharmacies and pharmacists, and he litigates on behalf of both, defending pharmacy malpractice claims. He also works with a pharmaceutical manufacturer, reviewing contractual and regulatory issues.

According to Rickert, for anyone considering a dual pharmacy/law degree, there are "a host of opportunities out there." Such professionals can work for drug or medical device companies, handling litigation issues and regulatory affairs, in corporate law departments, within federal government agencies such as the Food and Drug Administration, for pharmaceutical associations such as the National Association of Chain Drug Stores or state pharmacy associations, and at law firms with pharmacy or drug company clients as Rickert himself does. Attorney-pharmacists are employed at universities, schools of pharmacy teaching law, and within hospitals' legal departments. Academia offers other avenues. Rickert currently teaches the pharmacy law class at the University of Illinois. "It's interesting how many pharmacy students, who are otherwise stellar students, have trouble getting the law part down. So teaching this class is a challenge, but I enjoy the opportunity to work with the students, to learn from them and, hopefully, to influence them by what I do."

> "It's gratifying when we can make our voice heard and see that we're making a difference in the practice of pharmacy," she says. "Having a dual degree helps me understand the interplay between law and healthcare. That's especially important with the advent of powerful new drugs."
>
> Diane Darvey, PharmD, JD

Rickert is the immediate past president of the American Society for Pharmacy Law (ASPL), a group with approximately 800 members. Not all are pharmacist/attorneys but a good many are. Some are lawyers working on pharmacy matters and some are pharmacists with an interest in law.

The Pharmacist in Financial Industry

John P. Curran enjoyed being a community pharmacist but it has been over 20 years since he filled a prescription. He also enjoys being an investor with a pharmacist's perspective — a career that has been considerably more lucrative for him. As President and owner of Curran Capital Management, a New York City-based hedge fund, Curran trades healthcare stocks to make money for his clients. His $150-million fund, which specializes in drug and medical device companies and which he started 15 years ago, has done extraordinarily well, returning a compound annual rate of return of 40 percent.

A graduate of Fordham University College of Pharmacy and the University of Pittsburgh (MA and PhD in pharmaceutical economics), Curran worked as a Wall Street analyst specializing in drug companies and as manager of a pharmaceutical company's public policy research program before launching his own firm. Every step of the way, he has found his pharmacy background extremely valuable. "It's given me a knowledge of medicine and the ability to understand clinical reports and medical research papers," says Curran, 58.

On an average day, which begins at 5:30am with a marathon reading session of newspapers and research reports, Curran makes or receives 100 to 125 phone calls. Most are about trading ideas — a domestic company whose earnings overseas are due to a strong dollar, or one that's had a management shakeup or another that's come up with a great new drug. Calls average 22 seconds, he says, enough time to say yes, no or send more information. Before the stock market opens, he usually has breakfast with other money managers where they share ideas. From 9:00am until noon, Curran is glued to his computer, watching his stocks. There are thousands of stocks in the health universe but "in my solar system I keep track of about 50 names," Curran says.

After a business or social lunch, Curran, who is licensed as a pharmacist in New York and Pennsylvania, is back on the phone. He catches up with mail, signs legal documents and continues research. He averages three to five stock trades a day. "I only have seven to ten great ideas a year and I focus on them by making big bets on a few stocks," he says.

Soon after the stock market closes, Curran leaves the office, packing up some of the 30 sources he studies each week. "I'm basically an information prospector," he explains.

The Office Based Pharmacist

For two and a half years, Amy Barron, a 38-year-old mother of two, worked in a halfway house associated with Brantwood Pilgrim State Hospital, teaching mentally ill patients living skills so they could become independent. From there, she went to pharmacy school at St. Johns University in Queens, earning her bachelors degree in 1991. Today, Barron is an office-based pharmacist who works at Gentive Health Services, a home infusion service with offices in New York and New Jersey. At Barron's branch of Gentiva, five pharmacists supervise the care of approximately 500 patients ranging from infants to the elderly. Some are taking chemotherapy at home, others need IV antibiotics for an infection that oral medication isn't reaching, or other ailments that disallow conventional food intake. Barron is responsible for around 150 of these patients. Ninety percent of her work day is spent on the phone. She talks to physicians to get their orders, to patients to

see how they're doing on their medications, and to nurses who visit the patients in their homes. She evaluates lab results that come in over her fax machine to see if her patients' blood levels are stable and how the regime they're on is affecting them. For the other ten percent of her day, she monitors production, checking to see that the medicines for her patients have been prepared as directed, and referencing the literature to ensure the patient is being dosed correctly. In addition, she oversees distribution for the day — making sure the delivery tickets match the prescriptions and that the pumps and other supplies are in perfect working order.

It's easy to get caught up in the lives of your patients and in your workplace, Barron says, noting that she has done this often. From sharing lengthy phone time with these people, she says, "I have learned to be open to life and to embrace it."

The Pharmacist in an Advertising Agency

As Chief Strategic Officer at the Harrison & Star advertising agency in New York, Michelle Diamond-Sirota, RPh works with the firm's account teams to develop marketing plans and programs for the products of the agency's pharmaceutical clients. That could involve developing strategies, messages and tactical programs to reach the defined marketing objectives. An example was the selling idea or ad tagline developed for a drug indicated for the treatment of Multiple Sclerosis (MS), "Keeps on proving its power." This concept was arrived at based on the understanding that MS is a progressive and debilitating disease. Communicating that a treatment offers sustained efficacy in reducing relapses and disability in patients with MS is a powerful benefit.

Diamond, who earned a Bachelor's of Science in Pharmacy from Rutgers Pharmacy School in 1984, has worked as both a hospital and retail pharmacist and as a sales representative for a pharmaceutical company before joining the advertising world. She first worked as a senior account executive at Dugan Farley Communications where she worked with a pharmaceutical company on their cardiovascular and anti-infective business. Then she moved on to be an account supervisor at Thomas G. Ferguson Associates, and finally ended up at Harrison & Star where she is today. She first joined Harrison & Star in 1994, to work on the launch of a new oral medication for type 2 diabetes and was promoted into her current position last year. Harrison & Star, founded in 1987 employs about 150 people and is part of Omnicom, a large holding company of agencies.

Diamond is one of the few pharmacists within Omnicom's vast network. When launching the oral anti-diabetic, she often worked 15-hour days with a team consisting of copywriters and art directors developing brand messages and materials for the client's sales force, as well as educational materials for patients with type 2 diabetes. She also worked to solidify partnerships with constituents like the American Association of Diabetes Educators.

On a recent day, Diamond, who is 40, participated in a tactical brainstorming session from 9:00am to 11:00am, followed by an hour-long conference call with another client to review presentation materials for senior management. After a brief break, she was in a three-hour strategic brainstorming session for a third client. Summer is prime time for client planning, but her days are also spent preparing for new business opportunities. She's involved in at least one new "pitch" a month. And she regularly participates in internal strategic skills workshops to assist the agency's account people in fully

understanding the clients they represent. "In sales, I enjoyed meeting people but missed being part of a team," says Diamond "Working in advertising is demanding — you always have to be responsive to the client. It's a service business so you can't put something off to a more convenient time for you. But I wouldn't want to be doing anything else." She enjoys working with teams to develop creative ideas and likes the variety of working on different products. "Having both a pharmacy background and an industry sales background is a big plus."

These are just a few of the myriad career opportunities for pharmacists today. Whether you apply your pharmacy degree to a career as a market analyst, advertising executive or lawyer, a world of opportunity awaits today's students. Pharmacy training and practice provide today's practitioners with a solid background in health care and science. Coupled with specialized training in other areas such as law, finance, business, government, publicity or marketing, tomorrow's pharmacists can enjoy a broad range of rewarding and exciting careers. All it takes is a little risk and a lot of inspiration, motivation, and hard work. Shoot for the stars. The sky's the limit.

pharmacy benefit manager

A TRUE TALE

One day in 1978, three men receiving HIV therapy came to a small chain pharmacy in Alexandria, Virginia to pick up their medications. Michael Manolakis, PharmD, was the pharmacist on call. One of the men pulled out a credit card to pay for his medications. The second used co-insurance to reduce his out-of-pocket expense for the medicines. The third, who was receiving Medicaid assistance, had made many sacrifices to pay his part of the $800 a month drug cost.

Dr. Manolakis, who at the time was 27-years-old, was struck, even then, by the different payments each man faced. It made him wonder about the systems of medical support that provide more for those who have less, and how they are justified. The questions nagged at him until he finally went to the medical library and performed a literature search on the ethics of resource allocation. Though he found a great deal of literature in nursing and medicine, there was little or no research being done in pharmacy. For Manolakis, that scarcity sparked both interest and opportunity — an opportunity to return to school to pursue a graduate degree in bio-medical ethics.

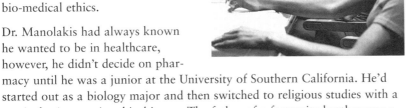

Dr. Manolakis had always known he wanted to be in healthcare, however, he didn't decide on pharmacy until he was a junior at the University of Southern California. He'd started out as a biology major and then switched to religious studies with a particular interest in ethical issues. The father of a fraternity brother was a pharmacist, and Dr. Manolakis was impressed by his clinical role which "progressively pushed the boundaries of practice."

After earning a bachelor's degree in religious studies in 1983, Dr. Manolakis stayed on at USC to pursue a PharmD degree, which he earned in 1987. After graduation, he took a job as a retail pharmacist in Washington DC, where he could also indulge his keen interest in politics. After working for two years as a retail pharmacist, the need to explore ethics further lead

Pharmacy Benefit Manager Checkpoint

Do you have an interest in and understanding of the financial side of healthcare?

Do you want to stretch well beyond clinical issues to understand all areas of a company?

Would you enjoy managing a group of people and developing team rapport?

If so, read on

Dr. Manolakis to return to graduate school. He did this while working part time as a pharmacist to pay the bills. In 1992 he had earned a PhD in ethics and philosophy with a concentration in bio-ethics from the University of Tennessee at Knoxville.

Dr. Manolakis was recruited by a Washington DC-based company to use his clinical skills in managing a program for state employees. The program's

medication costs were high because virtually anyone who wanted a product could get it. One example, Dr. Manolakis says, was the use of human growth hormone. He instituted a plan so that those persons who needed it for approved indications were covered under the plan, but where it was being used for an unapproved use, it would not be covered.

While his employer valued his extensive clinical background and keen interest in bio-ethics issues, after a couple of years in case management, he decided he wanted to explore the business side of the company. Thus, he took positions in sales support, marketing, and finally in sales, working his way up to his current title of Regional Director. Throughout his career, Dr. Manolakis has kept his interest in ethics and patient outcomes while focusing on learning how to run a business.

Profiling the job
While prescription drug benefits are now common in today's workplace, it was only in the late 1960s that insurers were asked to provide prescription drug coverage. This was a claims administration nightmare for insurance companies and it quickly became clear that a system had to be developed to effectively handle the high volume of claims coming in. This need spurred rapid growth of the pharmacy benefit management field over the next decade, and in the late 1980s, online electronic drug claims processing was introduced. By the 1990s, PBMs really became pharmacy care benefit managers, adding services that would produce savings and improve the quality of care.

Dr. Manolakis is currently Regional Director for a large pharmacy benefit management company. In this capacity he oversees the account teams that manage the pharmacy benefits for the Georgia Department of Community Health. His position requires him to interface with his client's top executives while managing seven people, and indirectly overseeing the pharmacy needs of 1.7 million citizens from the state of Georgia. Pharmacy benefit management companies (PBMs) handle some or all of the functions associated with administering and managing a prescription drug benefit program. These functions span the spectrum from claims processing and related administrative services, to management of the system's drug utilization review. They consult with employers, administrators of managed care organizations and third party administrators. Key benefit plan decisions include setting patient deductibles, negotiating prescription discounts, allotting annual maximums for high utilizing members, and determining co-payment arrangements. Since they have computer access to the files of their clients' patients, they can analyze drug prescribing to discover if beneficial and cost effective therapies have been correctly utilized.

"Unfortunately there is not enough money to pay for everything we'd like to reimburse for. As a result everyone in managed care faces the fundamental conflict of interest between holding down costs and meeting patient needs. Our struggle is to consistently make decisions that are ethically defensible and still in the best interest of the patient."

More than 90 percent of Health Maintenance Organizations used a PBM in the recent past for some aspect of health plan management according to a recent survey. Many PBMs are also involved with on-site education including developing such programs as "brown bag seminars," or prescription discussion meetings. These programs promote health and wellness by providing improved medication use.

Careers in this area are expected to grow over the next several years. New technology and use of the Internet will make some aspects of the PBM's work easier, but, with electronic transmission of data across the Web, patient confidentiality and privacy have emerged as key issues for those of us in this field, says Dr. Manolakis.

Selling the pharmacy benefit management service has forced Dr. Manolakis to understand the business side of pharmacy practice, especially how to negotiate and close business deals. It has also rewarded him with a relatively high salary — Dr. Manolakis' compensation is comparable to that of many business executives. He enjoys his job and the opportunity to develop professionally, and he also enjoys the hours. "It is a rare day that I don't get home for dinner," says Dr. Manolakis, who has two young boys, and a wife who is a pharmacist and independent consultant. The key challenge, he says, is "to identify a common ground with people whose priorities don't necessarily mesh with yours."

A day in the life

The workday for Dr. Manolakis usually begins around 7:30am. The first part of the day is spent catching up on correspondence. Once this is attended to, he heads into scheduled meetings for most of the remaining part of the day. The meetings revolve around issues of client needs, the needs of his company, and needs of his staff. Interspersed with the regular meetings are meetings with supervisors to review contract issues, new business development and financial aspects of the business.

"In managed care disease management is often looked upon as 'Big Brother', but on the positive side we can get a bird's eye view that a physician wouldn't be able to hone in on. Our service provides a safeguard to insure that everything about a patient is attended to correctly."

Mary Lynn Meyer, PharmD

When Dr. Manolakis and his team face a new issue, they spend time evaluating how it will impact program beneficiaries, pharmacy providers, and the client. They consider financial and clinical concerns and discuss how to effectively communicate plan changes. "Most pharmacists look at the financing systems from the outside in," says Dr. Manolakis. "I see things from a different perspective because I'm at the table with decision makers. I enjoy the challenges and opportunities associated with this role."

fast facts

What do you need?
- Strong business and management skills
- Ability to gather, analyze, and make decisions based on data
- Ability to multitask

How can I find out more?
- Search the Academy of Managed Care Pharmacy website at: www.amcp.org
- Identify and research individual PBM Websites
- Contact the Human Resources Departments at individual PBMs to see if there are internship or externship opportunities available

What's it take?
- A current, active license to practice pharmacy
- Bachelor of Science (BS) or Doctor of Pharmacy (PharmD) degree*
- Experience in business is preferred

Where will you practice?
- A corporate office setting

*Students graduating after Spring 2004 will be required to have a PharmD degree

"We're in the business of building relationships, of looking for synergies."

Mary Lynn
Meyer, PharmD

chapter twenty-three
poison control pharmacist

**Poison Control
Pharmacist
Checkpoint**

Are you able
to think fast
in critical
situations?

Do you have
deep drug
knowledge and
the ability to
communicate?

Can you handle
"emergency"
contact with
the public
and other
professionals?

If so, read on

A TRUE TALE

Winthrop University Hospital's Long Island Regional Poison Control and Drug Information Center, receives on average, 150 to 175 calls in every 24-hour period. Some are from health care professionals; the rest from any of the three million residents of Nassau and Suffolk counties who believe they or someone close to them have come in contact with something

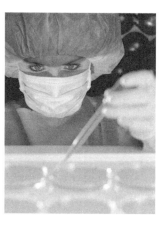

poisonous. Even though the Center saves thousands of lives every year, they estimate that in their service area approximately 15 people each year die from the poisons to which they are exposed.

There are approximately 75 regional poison control centers around the country that are open 24 hours a day, 7 days a week all year long. At least one certified specialist in poison information is at the center at all times, and back-up from a medical director or qualified designee, is just a pager away. The centers maintain comprehensive poison information resources and poisoning

management guidelines. Their managing directors are certified by the American Board of Medical Toxicology (ABMT) or by the American Board of Applied Toxicology (ABAT). The centers work closely with all poison treatment facilities (usually hospitals) and ambulance services in their region. All poison control centers (PCC) maintain records of all cases that are aggregated yearly by the American Association of Poison Control Centers in the National Data Collection System.

The specialty of poison control — which was established in the late 1970s with the introduction of universal standards and protocols — continues to grow because new chemicals and hazards are coming along every day.

Since January 1993, Thomas R. Caraccio, PharmD, now in his 40s, has been clinical manager of the center at Winthrop.

Dr. Caraccio decided to become a pharmacist when he was in high school in the Bronx working part-time at a local pharmacy. He was impressed by the meaningful contact he had with patients and his impact on their care. After graduating from high school in 1973, the New Yorker attended St. John's University College of Pharmacy. As soon as he graduated with a Bachelor of Science in Pharmacy degree in 1978, he attended the Massachusetts College of Pharmacy and Allied Health Sciences in Boston and received a PharmD degree from there in 1981.

During his schooling, Dr. Caraccio interned at several hospitals including Our Lady of Mercy and Montefiore in the Bronx; Beth Israel; Brigham and Women's; Tuft's New England Medical Center; and Lemmeul Shattuch in Boston, where he explored the idea of a career in hospital pharmacy. But while doing a rotation in drug information at Children's Hospital in Boston, he discovered the poison information center and was immediately captured by the combination of clinical practice and scientific application of knowledge.

His first full time job was as a Clinical Pharmacist at Norwalk Hospital in Norwalk, CT, from June 1981 to February 1982. He then moved to Nassau County Medical Center's Long Island Regional Poison Center in East Meadow, New York, as clinical coordinator; a job he held for 10 years before taking his current post in 1993 at Winthrop University Hospital in Mineola, New York.

Profiling the job

As Clinical Manager of Winthrop University Hospital's Long Island Regional Poison Control and Drug Information Center, Dr. Caraccio oversees its daily operations and manages a staff of 16 full-time employees including: a physician medical director, 13 nurse specialists in poison information, a nurse practitioner and secretarial and clerical staff. He also oversees the center's one million dollar budget and provides professional support, supervision, education and training for information specialists, nurses, pharmacists, medical students and residents in emergency medicine, pediatrics, preventive medicine, and clinical pathology. He regularly consults with health professionals, works on developing operational protocols and helps prepare fundraising efforts. He is also in charge of maintaining the center's communications network and public relations, coordinating monthly case reviews, teaching symposiums and research projects. Dr. Caraccio also co-edits a monthly newsletter and issues regular "ToxAlerts."

Did you know? The American Association of Poison Control Centers reports that in 1999 over 1.1 million children age five and under were exposed to potentially poisonous substances.

More than half of the calls received by the Center are exposures of children to poisons. Since children are constantly investigating the world around them, they often come in contact with items like household cleaners or their parents' medications. Older people are also at risk for poisoning because they get confused about different medications and don't know about the potential interactions. Further, they often can't read the small writing on drug labels.

Drug information calls with questions about aspirin and aceta-minophen are common, as are queries about oral prescription drugs, dietary supplements, OTC products, preparations containing lidocaine and dibucaine (anesthetic medicines), minoxidil, naproxen or ketoprofen, furniture polish, oil of wintergreen, many types of cleaners, lighter fluids, turpentine, paint solvents, windshield washer solutions, automobile antifreeze, rust removers, and pesticides.

A day in the life

On a typical day by 9:00am Dr. Caraccio is reviewing the charts of 10 to 15 patients hospitalized with drug-related problems. When he makes rounds with a physician, nurse, resident and students, he will be able to recommend a plan of care.

Next, Dr. Caraccio and his team review news that could affect the Center, such as the recall of a drug, a new antidote for methanol poisoning, or a potential chemical hazard from a propane truck tipping over. Several times every day information flows in from the Food & Drug Administration, product manufacturers and health departments. The communication is two way: The Center functions as the bio-surveillance unit for the health department and prepares relevant alerts, newsletters and website material.

Recently, an anonymous note was received at a local courthouse. It said the envelope contained anthrax bacillus. Dr. Caraccio had to decide if the center needed to prepare a news release to local hospitals and pharmacies.

Usually, Dr. Caraccio meets with different physicians and specialists over lunch and then, almost daily, from 1:00pm to 2:00pm he lectures students about some aspect of toxicology. He also spends time on research projects. A current research project involves an herbal product designed to prevent congestive heart failure. Another study involves reviewing cases to see how many herbal products have been involved in poisonings.

Dr. Caraccio has published clinical research on acetaminophen, cigarettes in children, ketorolac toxicity, gamma-hydroxy butyrate, and whole bowel irrigation as a treatment for poisonings, as well as the four Ecstasy's (herbal, chemical, liquid, OTC), nicotine dermal patch exposures, DEET insect repellant, solvent abuse, and carbon monoxide poisoning.

Throughout the day, poison control specialists consult him when they can't answer a caller's question. The team knows by heart the safeguards against West Nile virus, what to do if you are bitten by ticks or mosquitos, or that lobsters left in the trunk of a car overnight during the summer are not safe to eat. However, about half the time when he's consulted, Dr. Caraccio has to lead a research effort. Recently, a 16-year-old boy in a pet store was bitten by a Vietnamese centipede and his finger swelled to twice its normal size. The team contacted specialists at a local museum and pet distributor and then the Vietnam Consulate to no avail.

Sometimes, after taking a medical history and assessing the situation, a poison control specialist arranges to get a patient to a nearby hospital where an antidote can be administered and the patient can receive the

"We can't diagnose over the phone, but we do our best to ask the right questions, get a thorough understanding of the problem and give the caller vital information like what to do immediately. And problems are not always related to a child swallowing a poisonous substance by accident. For example, we've found interactions between herbals and prescriptions that many people are not aware of. In one two-month period, the center took 206 calls about toxic responses to herbal products."

monitoring he or she needs. But even if the patient stays home, the center's staff calls back to follow-up and make sure there are no problems.

At 4:00pm, Dr. Caraccio and his team begin to review all cases that came in during the day and discuss any significant hospital cases they are following. That two-hour review period is also prime time for call-ins. "Children are home and parents are distracted," he says.

Dr. Caraccio enjoys the variety of situations his work exposes him to. "I have the opportunity to work on different important areas like public and environmental problems as well as the P&T committee and with different people, including students." He finds gratifying the new, better treatments being developed. Syrup of ipecac used to be considered a good remedy for many poisons, he says, but in reality it only removes 30 percent of material in the stomach under optimal conditions. And if not given right away, it doesn't help much at all, he says. Dr. Caraccio also thoroughly enjoys writing drug-related articles and his yearly chapter in a book on poisoning and carrying out faculty appointments at New York College of Osteopathic Medicine, St. John's University College of Pharmacy and State University in New York at Stony Brook.

But he bemoans the fact that other practitioners are so busy that they don't have the time to be properly educated about antidotes, and the fact that not all the center's attempts have positive outcomes. One 52-year-old woman recently died, despite treatment, after taking an overdose of acetaminophen that led to liver failure and ultimately to multi-organ failure. She waited too long — 16 hours after taking it — before seeking medical help.

PATIENT POINT OF VIEW

A zookeeper was bitten by an African viper and even before the center was called his whole arm had swelled. Dr. Caraccio authorized a helicopter to meet him at the site and transport him to a facility where the anti-venom was stored. Later, when the man learned about his case — and how he was near death, he thanked the center staff profusely.

fast facts

<<<

What do you need?
- Ability to communicate with healthcare professionals and the public over the telephone during crisis circumstances
- Knowledge of crisis intervention techniques
- Data entry and documentation skills
- Strong knowledge and interest in pharmacology and toxicology

What's it take?
- A current, active license to practice pharmacy
- Bachelor of Science (BS) or Doctor of Pharmacy (PharmD) degree*
- Certification by the American Association of Poison Control Centers may be required within the first two years
- Course work in clinical toxicology is preferred
- One-year residency in poison-control pharmacy is preferred

Where will you practice?
- Poison control centers
- Hospitals
- Universities
- Consulting firms

*Students graduating after Spring 2004 will be required to have a PharmD degree

chapter twenty-four
primary care pharmacist

Primary Care Pharmacist Checkpoint

Are you more interested in a path with patient focus?

Would you enjoy the variety of seeing and evaluating patients across a large spectrum?

Are you interested in delivering more of a service rather than a product?

If so, read on

A TRUE TALE

Growing up in Central Valley, California, one of eight children whose parents ran a grocery store, William C. Gong, PharmD, FASHP, FCSHP

thought of pharmacists — when he thought of them at all — simply as dispensers of drugs or prescription fillers. Certainly, he didn't have that career in mind when he began San Jose State University in San Jose, California as a math major. But soon math became less interesting to him as chemistry appealed more, prompting him to switch his major. In 1970, he earned a Bachelor of Arts degree in chemistry.

Although he expected to go into pharmaceutical research and drug development, Dr. Gong got his first job in the lab of a technology company making napalm and rocket fuel for Air Force missiles during the Vietnam War. "It wasn't a particularly popular thing to do," says Dr. Gong, now 52. Subsequently, when Dr. Gong attended the University of Southern California School of Pharmacy in Los Angeles, he became interested in working directly with patients, and decided to subspecialize as a clinical pharmacist. Since 1982 he has been an Associate Professor of Clinical Pharmacy and Director for Residency and Fellowship Training at the USC School of Pharmacy and a primary care pharmacist at the Edward R. Royal Comprehensive Health Care Center in a general medicine clinic where he manages patients' chronic disease conditions.

> "I was less interested in the commercial aspect of pharmacy and more focused on patients. In primary care, we don't deal with a product so much as a service."

Profiling the job

As a primary care pharmacist at the Edward R. Royal Comprehensive Health Care Center, Dr. Gong is involved in evaluating physician-referred ambulatory patients and then caring for their drug needs. This requires his managing their drug therapy, ordering laboratory studies to determine their medication-related status, and adjusting the dosage of new or existing drugs as the patient's condition warrants.

Like any other healthcare provider, he documents his interventions in the patient's medical record. Once the patient has stabilized, Dr. Gong refers him back to the physician, who may call on Dr. Gong again as the need arises. Diabetes is one of the most common conditions among patients at the Center. Since it is a disease that requires close monitoring of the disease condition and medications, Dr. Gong sees some patients weekly or monthly.

As a member of the faculty at the USC School of Pharmacy, Dr. Gong implements curriculum, teaches pharmacy students, trains pharmacy residents and fellows, and develops healthcare services in the ambulatory care setting. In fact, one of his initiatives created his own job. He estimates that he works 50–60 hours per week and although the pay isn't as good as someone working in a store, he says he's not burnt out. "The patient interaction and the teaching keep me buzzing."

Helping patients get better, improving patient services and ushering students into significant leadership positions where they are able to implement changes are big pluses of the job. But the best thing about his work, Dr. Gong says, is that the nature of its schedule gives him control of his life. "I really like what I do and am not concerned with watching the clock. I enjoy seeing patients get well and they seem to know I'm playing a role in their recoveries."

Twenty-five years ago when Dr. Gong began his career track, few pharmacists had this type of practice. Though not widespread now, it is becoming more common. More and more pharmacists are performing clinical work and working as healthcare liaisons to physicians and medical groups. And an increasing number are getting more advanced training.

> *"I really like what I do and I am not concerned with watching the clock. I enjoy seeing patients get well and they seem to know I am playing a role in their recoveries."*

William C. Gong, PharmD, FASHP, FCSHP

A day in the life

Regular clinic hours run from 8:30am to 5:00pm. Upon arrival, he starts on rounds or medical conferences. Generally, Dr. Gong spends Monday, Tuesday, and Wednesday mornings in the clinic, where he sometimes cares for 10 to 15 patients a day and trains pharmacy students and residents. He consults with physicians, nurses and other healthcare providers throughout the day. Most of his patients, whose average age is 65, have diabetes, hypertension or other chronic diseases. Medications and insulin are the principal drugs he uses. On Thursdays

and Fridays, Dr. Gong is usually at the University, six miles from his office at the medical center, attending to administrative responsibilities, going to meetings, and supervising students. Dr. Gong works closely with administrators — setting up programs and services, and with physicians — regularly conferring about patients.

According to Dr. Gong, demand for primary care pharmacists is high, as managed care operations have more pharmacists involved with primary care and medication monitoring. According to Dr. Gong, primary care pharmacy is one of the fastest growing areas not only in pharmacy, but in all of healthcare. Gong, who has five children, says he would be very happy to have any or all of them become a pharmacist.

PATIENT POINT OF VIEW

The 84-year-old man with diabetes had been one of Dr. Gong's first patients when he began practicing 25 years ago. The patient came in repeatedly through the years and reminded Dr. Gong's student that he'd known Dr. Gong when he was a "student." Dr. Gong sat and listened as the man told him how he was feeling, and what was happening with his family. The man's wife presented the pharmacist with some home-baked cookies. "You spend time with us," they told him. "We never feel you're in a rush and we always feel you care."

fast facts

What do you need?
- Ability to work alongside physicians and nurses as part of a primary healthcare team
- Written and oral communication skills
- Desire to be directly involved in patient care

What's it take?
- A current, active license to practice pharmacy
- Bachelor of Science (BS) or Doctor of Pharmacy (PharmD) degree*
- Completion of a generalized residency followed by a specialized residency (in either primary care, internal medicine or family practice) is preferred

Where will you practice?
- General internal medicine clinics
- Primary care clinics
- Family medicine clinics
- Specialty clinics
- Universities

*Students graduating after Spring 2004 will be required to have a PharmD degree

chapter twenty-five
psychiatric pharmacist

**Psychiatric
Pharmacist
Checkpoint**

Are you able to
respect mentally
ill people and
empathize with
their problems?

Do you exude
self-confidence?

Do you have
the patience to
explain phar-
macotherapy
in great detail?

If so, read on

A TRUE TALE

Each year, 23 percent of adult Americans suffer from diagnosable mental
disorders, of which anxiety disorders are the most common. Four of the ten
leading causes of disability in the United States are mental disorders and
approximately a fourth of total hospital admissions in the U.S. are psychiatric admissions.

As startling as these statistics may seem, the bright side is that ongoing
research in this area has led to increasingly successful treatment for a growing

number of affected people. Most people with
mental illness recover well with appropriate
ongoing treatment and support. On the team
for treating these types of conditions are
psychiatric pharmacists like Sara Grimsley
Augustin, PharmD, BCPP.

No one in Sara Grimsley Augustin's family
ever had any connection to pharmacy. Her
mom is a teacher and her dad is a game
warden. Her stepfather is an accountant and
her stepmother is a banker. But the 36-year-
old, eldest of three girls and native of the
small town of Waverly, Tennessee was always
interested in science. She chose pharmacy, among the various healthcare related
professions she was considering, during her first year of undergraduate studies
at the University of Tennessee at Knoxville. Although that choice was made
rather quickly, as she was feeling pressure to declare a major, she's never
been sorry. "Pharmacy turned out to be the perfect career choice for me."

Dr. Augustin enrolled in Mercer University Southern School of Pharmacy in
Atlanta in 1985. In 1989, she received her doctorate degree in pharmacy
(while working for three years part-time at Boyles Drug Company in Atlanta)
and in the next year completed a post-doctoral residency in psychiatric
pharmacy there. Since then she has been on the faculty. She became a board
certified psychiatric pharmacist (BCPP) in February 1997.

Profiling the job

It wasn't until her last year of pharmacy school, during her clinical psychiatry
clerkship, that Dr. Augustin found her true niche in pharmacy: dealing with
the pharmaceutical care needs of mentally ill patients. Although she had

always been fascinated by psychology and psychiatry, she wasn't previously aware of this area of specialization in pharmacy. She quickly learned about the many activities psychiatric pharmacists can be involved in and realized this was the specialty for her. "Psychiatric pharmacists can have a real impact on patients, providing education about medications, monitoring for side effects of medications, and making recommendations to improve the outcomes of drug therapy," she says. A big problem in the area of psychiatry is that mentally ill individuals often stop taking the medications, which are necessary for the control of chronic illnesses, such as schizophrenia and bipolar disorder. Whether because of adverse effects, poor understanding of a medication's potential benefits, or poor recognition of their illness, non-compliance signals a gap in treatment. Pharmacists can play a vital role in filling this gap by identifying and addressing reasons for the discontinuation of pharmacotherapy, leading cause of relapse of mental illness and hospitalization.

> "In the past decade there has been an explosion in the number of medications available to treat psychiatric disorders, as well as an increased awareness about the numbers of people suffering from these illnesses."

A day in the life

Dr. Augustin's area of practice in psychiatric pharmacy involves a lot of teaching. In fact, much of her week is devoted to teaching fourth-year pharmacy students in the clinical psychiatry clerkship program at the Georgia Regional Hospital of Atlanta, a 250-bed state psychiatric facility. This is an elective advanced practice experience, and four to six students usually sign up for the clerkship she precepts each five-week session. While Dr. Augustin works for the pharmacy school, she uses the hospital, which is 20 minutes away, as a training site. Her students go there every day; Dr. Augustin meets them there several days a week. Under her direction, students become experienced at interacting with and providing medication counseling to the psychiatric patients there. They also learn to work with members of the treatment team (comprising psychiatrists, psychologists, nurses, social workers, activity therapists, and other staff) to develop and carry out the individualized treatment plan for each patient. Various units throughout the hospital are designated for treating specialized psychiatric populations, such as children, adolescents, developmentally disabled clients, the elderly, and those with substance abuse problems. Currently, the adult forensic psychiatry units are frequently utilized for student clerkship training. These units are devoted to treating patients with legal issues, such as those found not guilty of a crime for reasons of insanity or those deemed incompetent to stand trial because of their mental illness. "One of the most important things students learn on this rotation is to give up the stereotypic fears about people who are mentally ill. They quickly realize that even psychotic criminals are human beings with medically treatable conditions and deserve to be dealt with honestly, respectfully and compassionately."

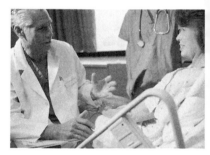

Other activities of the clerkship include conducting patient medication education groups and attending group meetings on specific topics, such as depression, anxiety disorders, substance abuse, schizophrenia, and epilepsy, during which students present patient cases for discussion. These meetings are held two to three times weekly with Dr. Augustin or her colleague.

Dr. Augustin also teaches a number of psychiatry and neurology-related courses to second and third-year students. Her lecture topics include obsessive-compulsive disorder, panic disorder, post-traumatic stress disorder, social anxiety disorder, postpartum depression, premenstrual dysphoric disorder, insomnia, narcolepsy, anorexia and bulimia nervosa, obesity, weight loss and seizure disorders. She is faculty coordinator for the required clinical pharmacokinetics course and teaches the pharmacokinetics of antidepressants, lithium, and anticonvulsants in that course. Dr. Augustin also teaches an elective substance abuse course, in which she lectures on alcoholism, drug testing, and abuse of substances such as cocaine, amphetamines, ecstasy, heroin, inhalants, anabolic steroids, and prescription medications.

Because she teaches different courses, Dr. Augustin's classroom teaching load is much heavier at certain times of the year. Sometimes she teaches four hours a day four days a week, sometimes she doesn't teach for weeks. "I'm on whenever my topic comes up," she says. There are about 520 pharmacy students in the pharmacy program. Dr. Augustin will ultimately teach every one of them.

With such a focus on teaching psychiatric pharmacy, Dr. Augustin's work largely reflects that of an academic. She also conducts research, writes papers for publication in professional pharmacy journals and textbooks, and serves on various committees of the pharmacy school, such as the Curriculum Committee, the Admissions Interview Committee, and the Honors Awards and Scholarships Committee. But the part she likes best is teaching psychiatric issues, particularly helping students gain a better understanding of various mental illnesses and their treatments. Dr. Augustin has enormous freedom, doesn't overwork ("I probably average 45 hours a week," she says), has excellent benefits and vacation (22 days a year), and is constantly stimulated. "My job allows me to continue learning. I must keep up with what is current."

Dr. Augustin is a member of several professional pharmacy organizations, using her expertise in psychiatry to serve as a reviewer for manuscripts submitted for publication in a variety of pharmacy journals. She is a member of the national Board of Pharmaceutical Specialties Council on Psychiatric Pharmacy, which is responsible for developing and administering standards for board certification in psychiatric pharmacy. There are currently 352 board certified psychiatric pharmacists (BCPP) around the world; she predicts this number will grow as more people realize the value of this level of specialty practice.

Dr. Augustin, recently married to a research scientist with a pharmaceutical company, also spends one morning a week as a clinical pharmacy consultant to the neurobehavioral unit — a private brain injury rehabilitation program. The patients in this program have severe psychiatric and behavioral problems, secondary to traumatic brain injuries most commonly due to car accidents, falls, or assaults. "We use a combination of medications and behavioral therapies to control their psychiatric symptoms so they can continue with other aspects of their rehabilitation. The effects of psychiatric medications in patients with brain injuries are often very different from what we see in people without such injuries, so this can be a very challenging population to treat." The 10 to 15 patients in this small program may remain several months to several years.

"Years ago, electroconvulsive therapy and non-pharmacological treatments were shots in the dark. While they were very effective for some disorders, thanks to years of research there are now many chances to be effectively treated in a less invasive way."

PATIENT POINT OF VIEW

The 20-year-old schizophrenic male had been hearing voices telling him to kill family members and harm himself. He thought the television and radio personalities were talking to and about him and he had become paranoid about everyone. He'd been on the acute psychiatric unit for several weeks and had initially resisted taking medication because he thought the care providers were trying to poison him. When finally convinced to try an antipsychotic medication, he suffered distressing side effects (acute muscle spasms and hand tremors). Interpreting this experience as proof the medication was poison, the young man refused to take any more. Dr. Augustin worked with the patient, finally convincing him to try another antipsychotic medication, and within a short time his psychosis resolved. Shortly thereafter, he was discharged from the hospital and was able to get his first real job. He and his family were educated about schizophrenia and the importance of medications in its treatment. Dr. Augustin cites this as an instance in which a psychiatric pharmacist can really make a difference in a patient's life.

>>> # fast facts

What do you need?
- Ability to work as part of a multidisciplinary team
- A broad knowledge of psychiatric disorders and treatments
- A interest in interacting with psychiatric patients

What's it take?
- A current, active license to practice pharmacy
- Bachelor of Science (BS) or Doctor of Pharmacy (PharmD) degree*
- One-year residency in psychiatric pharmacy is preferred
- Certification as a Board Certified Psychiatric Pharmacist (BCPP) is preferred

Where will you practice?
- Psychiatric hospitals
- Hospitals
- Universities
- Home health care
- Nursing home care
- Acute care facilities
- Ambulatory care facilities

*Students graduating after Spring 2004 will be required to have a PharmD degree

chapter twenty-six
public health service pharmacist

A TRUE TALE

James Bresette, PharmD, grew up in a military family. By the time he went to college, he had lived in Westhampton, NY, Tripoli, Libya, Ramstein, Germany, Plattsburg, New York, Sacramento, California, and Central Florida. But his upbringing was just a primer for a future that would be full of diversity. After attending The Citadel on a four-year ROTC scholarship, he received an undergraduate degree in chemistry and was commissioned as a second lieutenant in the United States Air Force. Although he initially began his Air Force career as a missile crew commander, he eventually found himself working at the ultra-secret National Security Agency. Working with computer scientists and mathematicians in developing encrypted nuclear weapons code

components. He and his team also formulated and interpreted national nuclear command and control policy. But soon after he entrenched himself in this field, he had a notion that led him in a different direction.

In 1992, with less than nine years to retirement, he left the Air Force for pharmacy school. After receiving his PharmD degree from the University of Maryland, Dr. Bresette was commissioned as a lieutenant in the United States Public Health Service (USPHS) and assigned to the Indian Health Service (IHS) at the Ft. Peck Reservation. Remote by Maryland standards, Ft. Peck is tucked into Montana's northeast corner sixty miles south of Saskatchewan and eighty miles west of North Dakota. Home to nearly ten thousand Assiniboine and Sioux Indians, Ft. Peck's two health clinics employ five pharmacists when fully staffed. Stationed at the clinic in Wolf Point, Dr. Bresette at first worked with another pharmacist and a technician. As a "frontier pharmacist" Dr. Bresette says it was necessary to function from "day one" providing primary care, ascertaining appropriate drug therapy for each patient, and counseling all patients on their medications. When the other pharmacist transferred, counseling every patient (an IHS hallmark), became extremely difficult. Committed to giving his patients his best, Dr. Bresette recalled a challenge he had once heard from Rear Admiral

Public Health Service Pharmacist Checkpoint

Do you consider your-self a generalist in health not just limited to pharmacy?

Would you appreciate a "spiritual engagement" working in a closed community?

Are you willing to take on responsibility outside a narrow job description?

If so, read on

Fred Paavola, the USPHS Chief Pharmacist Officer, to "think outside the box and if that does not work, create a new box." Soon Dr. Bresette was teaching a course to get Ft. Peck's technicians certified, working with a drug company to install satellite televised patient health information in the pharmacy waiting area, and even bringing robotics to Ft. Peck with one of the first two automated prescription filling units used in IHS.

Dispensing, however, did not preclude pharmaceutical care. Recognizing that a large number of beta-2 agonist metered dose inhalers were being dispensed, Dr. Bresette began to collect data and study the situation. After identifying excessively high asthma rates, he authored and received an American Pharmaceutical Association grant to expand asthma care services. Eventually, this led to working within the community to increase asthma awareness and culminated in an asthma camp he founded and directed. He quickly adds, "I received a lot of help from parents, business leaders, tribal leaders and elders, and IHS professionals who all invested their time and talent to see it succeed."

When an opportunity arose to start clinical pharmacy services in the nation's highest security federal prison, Dr. Bresette applied for the position. After two years with the IHS, he was reassigned to the Federal Bureau of Prisons, another agency open to PHS health professionals. As the chief pharmacist, he ran the in-house pharmacy for the 400 prisoners in the penitentiary. All prison staff respond immediately when inmate disturbances occur and a staff member activates his or her body alarm. To be ready for this, Dr. Bresette received six weeks of training in correctional techniques that included psychology, negotiating and confrontation avoidance, self-defense, and firearms training. Describing the training as a perfect blend of academics, role-playing, and hands on training, Dr. Bresette found the experience at the Federal Law Enforcement Training Center stimulating and unique. He was elected class president by his peers and graduated with honors.

Although for Dr. Bresette pharmacy practice in a correctional facility eventually became routine, he found it rewarding attending to patients with AIDS, tuberculosis, and a variety of chronic diseases. After a year, he was confident he would find something that would continue to challenge him professionally. "The Public Health Service is a smorgasbord of opportunities and cool jobs!" he says. While interviewing at the National Institutes of Health, he stopped by IHS headquarters and learned of a position as deputy director for clinical and preventative services. "I wasn't readily thinking of hanging up my 'clinical' cleats and coaching from the sidelines, but this seemed to be a once-in-a-career opportunity to know you made a difference," says Dr. Bresette.

The office Director, a practicing physician and assistant surgeon general, was looking to synergize the professions of medicine and pharmacy as well as coordinate clinical services and emphasize preventive care throughout the IHS. Dr. Bressette, with his personal commitment to improving the health of American Indians and Alaska Natives and his host of accomplishments (he was the 2000 PHS Clinical Pharmacist of the Year and the 2001 recipient of the Vice Admiral C. Everett Koop Award), seemed like the right fit.

Profiling the job

The U.S. Public Health Service (PHS) is one of the nation's largest employers of pharmacists. Assignments within the PHS include the Agency for Healthcare Research and Quality, the Bureau of Prisons, the Centers for Disease Control and Prevention, the Food and Drug Administration (FDA), the Centers for Medicare and Medicaid Services (formerly the Health Care Financing Administration), National Institutes of Health, the Office of Emergency Preparedness, the Immigration and Naturalization Service, the Substance Abuse and Mental Health Services Administration, the U.S. Agency for International Development, the Agency for Toxic Substances and Disease Registry, the U.S. Coast Guard, the Health Resources Services Administration, and the Indian Health Service.

The FDA, for example, employs over 300 pharmacists in 150 locations, working in pharmacology, radiopharmacology, toxicology and pharmacokinetics to ensure the safety and efficacy of drugs. These pharmacists deal with new drug applications and adverse event reports, conduct field inspections,

Did you know?
Since its creation in 1798, the U.S. Public Health Service has continually redirected its resources to meet the changing needs of the nation. Two centuries ago, the focus was the Merchant Marines; in the 1800s, arriving immigrants; in the early 1900s, contagious disease.

and serve on expert advisory committees and review panels. Many new pharmacy graduates begin in the Indian Health Service, a branch of the Public Health Service, which employs more than 500 pharmacists and provides clinical pharmacy services to 1.5 million American Indians and Alaska Natives in 34 states.

A day in the life

By 7:00am on days he isn't traveling, Dr. Bresette is deep into answering the 30 to 40 that have surfaced overnight and will continue throughout the day. Then he begins meetings with some of the 40 staffers who report to him, perhaps planning alcohol or mental health programs, or programs for chronic conditions like diabetes — a disease that affects three to four times more Native Americans than Caucasians. He might also spend time working on a diabetes grant or determining how to implement new programs and get money into the field.

"There's a big difference between the need and what we're able to provide. We're allocated at 55 percent of what most health insurance plans provide or about half what a Federal employee is entitled to, so we have to carefully manage care and aggressively seek out strategic partnerships with foundations and other federal agencies."

Typically, on days he's at headquarters in Rockville, Maryland, he attends two to four meetings within IHS and other federal agencies, in addition to another half-dozen over the phone. Seven to ten days a month he is on the road, auditing one of the fifty hospitals, several hundred clinics, health centers and health stations around the country, or attending meetings with leaders of the nearly 570 federally recognized tribes to assess the need for new programs and the health status of the community. Roughly half the tribes have transferred responsibility for health programs to tribal management. "It provides innovative solutions to some uncommon health care problems. In Alaska, 200 villages have clinics manned by community health aides who communicate with physicians by radio and telemedicine. For the rest, we're like a management cooperative," he says.

His team also oversees payments for contract health services and makes arrangements with Veteran's Administration hospitals and the Department of Defense. The IHS bills Medicare and Medicaid about $400 million a year, but is financially responsible for covering the difference.

Although civilian and commissioned corps PHS pharmacists earn less than they would in private industry to start, generous loan repayment programs, excellent federal employee benefits, salaries that do not plateau as they sometimes do in the private sector, up to 30 days vacation a year, bonus pays, tax-deferred income, travel opportunities, and the ability to retire after 20 to 30 years at half to three fourths base pay make the PHS very attractive. More important, says Dr. Bresette, "is the satisfaction of knowing you're doing good things for people, that they benefit from what you do." Other benefits are less tangible, but no less important. He can barely contain his enthusiasm when he talks about how he will be part of the PHS Commissioned Corps Readiness Force team that will provide medical support and disaster response for the 2002 Winter Olympics in Salt Lake City.

Dr. Bresette said he feels blessed to have career opportunities that offer so much intellectual growth, spiritual fulfillment, and a tie to his past. "My father was born on the Red Cliff reservation in northern Wisconsin and my grandfather attended the Carlisle Indian Academy with Jim Thorpe. My grandfather left the reservation for better economic opportunities and my father left to attend college, but never finished because he flew bombers over North Africa and Europe in World War II," says Dr. Bresette. "Graduating from college and working for Native American people is simply coming full circle."

PATIENT POINT OF VIEW

In his first capacity as a Public Health Service pharmacist assigned to the IHS, Dr. Bresette did more than keep the pharmacy open long after its official 4:30pm close. He recalls one patient thanking him: "Whenever there was anyone in the waiting room, you stayed until we were all taken care of." Another patient credits him for mobilizing the community with limited resources to "donate transportation and merchandise to raise money to start an asthma camp. He even held a community yard sale on his front lawn." Upon leaving Ft. Peck, patients' gifts included a handmade star-quilt, belt buckle, blanket, a sweat lodge ceremony, well wishes, and "plenty of hugs." Dr. Bresette says it inspires you to work harder and "these are the fringe benefits you can't get anywhere else."

"We (the IHS) are a trust entity. We offer a prepaid health insurance program for American Indians and Alaskan Natives."

James Bresette, PharmD

What do you need?
- ○ Commitment to public health
- ○ Willingness to work with medically underserved populations
- ○ Ability to take on a variety of administrative and clinical roles

What's it take?
- ○ A current, active license to practice pharmacy
- ○ Bachelor of Science (BS) or Doctor of Pharmacy (PharmD) degree*

Where will you practice?
- ○ Agency for Healthcare Research Quality
- ○ Bureau of Prisons
- ○ Centers for Disease Control and Prevention
- ○ Food and Drug Administration (FDA)
- ○ Health Care Financing Administration
- ○ National Institutes of Health
- ○ Office of Emergency Preparedness
- ○ Immigration and Naturalization Service
- ○ Substance Abuse and Mental Health Services Administration
- ○ US Agency for International Development
- ○ US Coast Guard
- ○ Indian Health Service

*Students graduating after Spring 2004 will be required to have a PharmD degree

chapter twenty-seven
regulatory pharmacist

A TRUE TALE

At the American Pharmaceutical Association in Washington DC, the national professional society of pharmacists, more than 100 staffers work to represent pharmacists, including representing the profession's interests to Congress and other law making bodies, to interpret how those laws impact pharmacists and to translate those findings to the pharmacy community. As group director for policy and advocacy since July 1999, Susan C. Winckler, RPh, JD, is on the front lines. "Instead of explaining complex medication therapy to patients, I try to explain pharmacy to non-pharmacists," she says.

It seemed a natural fit for the 32-year-old native of Sioux City, Iowa. Both her parents are pharmacists (as are an uncle and cousin in community practice) at their small, family-run pharmaceutical manufacturing company. The company specializes in medical cosmetics. "It was an easy decision for me to go to pharmacy school because I had seen the practice my whole life," Winckler says.

Winckler worked at a community pharmacy while attending the University of Iowa College of Pharmacy. After earning a Bachelor of Science in 1992, she decided to apply for an internship at the Iowa Pharmacists Association. "I sensed that non-traditional work using my pharmacy education was where I should be," she says.

After her internship with the Iowa Pharmacists Association, Winckler worked for a year devising cost containment measures to guide people who process claims for the Iowa Medicaid department. She was the first pharmacist at her company and her role evolved into explaining the needs of pharmacists to claims processors and sharing the fundamentals of the Medicaid program to fellow pharmacists and physicians.

Eventually she joined the APhA as manager of special projects, which included drug utilization review, immunization initiatives' and practice affairs. Here, in addition to monitoring and evaluating pharmacy and health care professional and policy issues, she worked in conjunction with other

**Regulatory
Pharmacist
Checkpoint**

Do you enjoy
multi-tasking?

Can you
analyze an
issue both
quickly and
completely?

Can you
articulate a
position and
speak on a
number of
different issues?

If so, read on

APhA departments and other pharmacy and health organizations on matters of professional, scientific, economic and government affairs. She also developed and managed the department's budget.

In May 1997 she was promoted to director of policy and legislation and two years later to her current post, reporting to the senior vice president of policy planning and communications. While holding both of these jobs, she attended Georgetown University Law Center in Washington, DC, and in February 2001 received her law degree. "I loved law school and learned to think like a lawyer. But I am a pharmacist first."

"I really enjoy working with different organizations, bringing people and perspectives together and helping to figure out directions for the profession. It's an honor being being a voice for pharmacists."

Profiling the job

The APhA's highest priorities now revolve around securing payment — particularly from Medicare and Medicaid. Another priority is to provide resources to state associations to help make certain functions such as administering immunizations for example, authorized for reimbursement in the state. The Association also works to ensure that pharmacists have the time to care for patients by trying to improve the quality of their work life. Winckler's job is as an ambassador and arbitrator. "I work to make sure that pharmacists are in situations where they can provide these services without sacrificing quality of work life. My job is to try to lighten their burden of bureaucracy by watching new regulations and laws closely to see what effects they might have on practice." For example, in December 2000, a bill that sought to protect patient health information, while laudable in its intentions, turned out to be one that could unduly burden pharmacists. One element of the bill required written consent before a pharmacist could prepare a prescription. While that posed no problem for the patient bringing in the prescription along with his or her consent, there can be problems if the physician calls in a prescription or a patient is new to the physician or pharmacy. Pharmacists, spurred by the APhA, convinced the secretary of the Department of Health and Human Services to reopen the discussion period for thirty days.

A day in the life

Winckler is on the road virtually all the time. She travels to meetings to update pharmacists in the latest congressional legislation and to share with non-pharmacists the pharmacists' perspective on certain issues. In spring 2001, not a week went by when she wasn't meeting with senior advocacy groups or general policy makers or congressional staff or regulatory agencies to talk about how to structure the Medicare pharmacy benefit or what Congress can do about the severe pharmacist shortage. In addition to outside meetings, Winckler periodically gets together with her administrative coordinator and three colleagues, to stay abreast of what is happening in the other divisions. "For me to advocate and to set an advocacy agenda I need to know what our members, officers and board of trustees think." Winckler also regularly meets with representatives from other pharmacy and health advocacy groups where agendas may overlap. "The way you get things done in this city is by working together," she says.

On mornings when she is based at headquarters, Winckler usually arrives at work by 8:00am. First she reads and responds to email. Before she plunges into an interdepartmental or external meeting she meets with her team "to see where we are and where we are going." Here she writes a one-or two-page statement outlining where APhA is on specific issues and positions she'll take on these issues.

Every Wednesday afternoon there's a briefing with other department heads to see where projects already overlap — or could. And there are annual policy development meetings with APhA's House of Delegates. Because she is a press representative for APhA, Winckler meets regularly with the public relations team and talks with reporters on average twice a week.

Before Winckler leaves for the day, she writes her memos and position papers. She has written about such wide-ranging subjects as whether new regulations in diabetes education will improve care, whether paperless labeling is a good idea, how direct-to-consumer advertising can benefit the pharmacist, and the prescription-to-OTC switch from the pharmacists' perspective. Other topics on her agenda include: the regulation of dietary supplements, how foreign imports work as a 'Band-Aid' to high medication costs, Internet pharmacy, the pharmacist's role in emergency contraception, and pain management. Representing the association, she has appeared on *CNN, Good Morning America, CNN Financial News,* and the *CBS Evening News.* "These are not horribly long days in comparison to when I was going to law school and working at the same time, but the hours are substantial," she notes. "It's the kind of road warrior life that would be difficult if I had kids," adds Winckler who was recently engaged.

Although a law degree is not necessary to her job, Winckler says it has been very helpful. She sees job security in the fact that Congress meets every year with the potential to make things happen that need responding to. She is satisfied with the pay (although "association work is not where you'll make a lot of money" she cautions). Another caveat: Since there is relatively no patient contact, pharmacists looking for that type of work should not consider the regulatory field. But Winckler loves what she does and finds it very satisfying — even exhilarating when someone else adopts a position she has been advocating.

PATIENT POINT OF VIEW
Pharmacists take the time to send in letters with their comments. One wrote congratulating Winckler, reaffirming that she and the Association were "on point and headed in the right direction." The letter continued: "Pharmacists support the way you are focusing on the Medicare pharmacy benefit issue, changing the dialogue from paying for product to paying for product and services that make those products work." The enthusiastic pharmacist noted, "Largely because of your efforts, in the last session of Congress there were four bills proposing payment for pharmacy services."

fast facts

What do you need?

- Project management/organizational skills
- Negotiation and communication skills
- Understanding of the scientific and technical background of products
- Willingness to keep up to date with regulatory policies and procedures

What's it take?

- Current, active license to practice pharmacy is helpful, but not necessary
- Two years' preprofessional experience, or PharmD degree
  (PharmD may not be required)

Where will you practice?

- Associations
- Government
- Consulting companies
- Pharmaceutical companies
- Universities

chapter twenty-eight
veterinary pharmacist

Veterinary Pharmacist Checkpoint

Are you eager for an unconventional career experience?

Do you feel comfortable around animals?

Are you well-versed and excited about expanding your knowledge in pharmacology for different animal species?

If so, read on

A TRUE TALE

Each year, pet owners spend more than $3 billion to maintain the health of their animals. The veterinary pharmacist is indispensable as a provider of animal health care. The pharmacists' knowledge of drugs, their stability, and their mechanisms of action and administration, may mean the difference in the outcome for a sick or injured animal.

Don Michalski, RPh, MS, ardently believes that a special relationship exists between human beings and members of the animal kingdom. Michalski is the Director of Pharmacy at the University of Wisconsin Veterinary School. He is responsible for developing the drug distribution system, including purchasing and contract management. I'm the "keeper of the keys," the 55-year-old Michalski states.

Michalski grew up surrounded by animals, on a dairy farm near a small, rural town in northern Wisconsin. For a while he considered careers in meteorology or agricultural research. Along the way, however, goaded by his father's exhortations to find a career where he could be his own boss, Michalski discovered pharmacy.

He received a Bachelor's degree in pharmacy from the University of Wisconsin in 1968, and practiced in a private hospital in Milwaukee for four years. He then returned to the University of Wisconsin for a residency and Master's degree in hospital pharmacy. Later he moved to the 350-bed Swedish American Animal Hospital in Illinois as an associate director.

Profiling the job

Michalski arrived at the University of Wisconsin in March 1983, the year the Center began seeing patients. He estimates that nearly 1,000 animals were seen that first year. Now, there are 50 clinical faculty members and 25 esidents. Last year the center cared for 16,000 animals. In addition to Michalski, there is one other full-time pharmacist, one part-time pharmacist, three technicians and two office staff that work in the purchasing office.

"What's different about veterinary pharmacy is that rather than dealing with the patient, you most often deal with the owner," says Michalski. "In that sense, it's very much like a pediatric population where your client is mom or dad." The therapy is also different since many of the diseases are different. A lot of diseases do, however, parallel human illnesses. Michalski and his staff regularly see animals for cancer, ophthamological problems, kidney transplants, cardiac conditions, gastrointestinal problems, orthopedic difficulties, and behavioral problems. There are also theriogenology specialists to handle artificial insemination, and neonatologists to care for foals. Most of the patients are beloved "companion animals," but the staff also sees dairy cattle, snakes, horses, llama, goats, pigs and other species. Few of the medications or medical services are covered by insurance. Bills can easily soar to $10,000 or more.

> "The Veterinary School at the University of Wisconsin is every bit like a human hospital except that the patients are four-legged or winged or they have no legs at all."

A day in the life

Michalski's day begins early. Usually, by 6:00am he is reviewing the previous night's activities and attending to administrative duties. By midday, he and the staff are busy preparing antibiotics, cardiac and chemotherapy injections for horses and cattle, and flavored oral therapies for dogs, cats and exotic species. Birds, snakes, gerbils and rabbits require special palate formulations. Often they use butter or liver sausage as a base to entice the animals to take their medicine. He also reformulates tablets and capsules and prepares topical gels.

Did you know?
Dogs get cancer at roughly the same rate as humans, while cats get fewer cancers. Cancer accounts for almost half of the deaths of pets over 10 years of age.

On a typical day, the staff prepares about 200 prescriptions. Some days are non-stop; others are slower. Once Michalski and his staff readied more than 300 syringes in a day. The most common drugs his center dispenses are heartworm preventatives and anti-parasite drugs, antibiotics and hormone therapy. A growing therapeutic area in veterinary pharmacy, Michalski says is pain management. His arsenal also runs to the unusual: Michalski recently administered a $50,000 dosage of surfactant for an immature calf's lungs. The calf was being used for a cloning project. The advances in biotechnology and xenobiology could produce an expanded role for the care of such super-animals that will be used as living product and organ factories.

The staff also prepares dosages for double-blind research studies, teaches veterinary and pharmacy students, and manages clerkships. Approximately two thirds of students take the veterinary pharmacy elective.

One aspect of the job that Michalski treasures most is the feeling of being highly valued. While accompanied by a technician on his way to check the six to 15 patients in the post-operative critical care unit, he is often barraged with questions from other healthcare workers or animal owners.

The casual consultations continue as Michalski makes his way to the large animal unit where he checks the medications of the five to 20 animals in residence there. The questions continue to flow in over the two windows at the Pharmacy. Perhaps five to 10 calls a day are received from veterinarians around the state and country. Often he has many requests for information and help from the 40 veterinary students on rotation and the 20 residents dispatched to the pharmacy to pick up drugs along with lessons about dosages and new therapies.

Other positive aspects of the job, he says, are the variety of conditions he encounters and the people with whom he works. Together, they more than makes up for a salary that is lower than most other areas of pharmacy — and the long hours. Michalski is called in on weekends a few times a month when residents need support.

Being a veterinary pharmacist has convinced him of the importance of the human-animal bond. "I know that some students decide to go into veterinary pharmacy for the love of a pet. I've seen many people stricken with grief over the loss of their animal. I've also seen brusque individuals become soft and sweet around their animals. My work has really taught me about the love between humans and their animals."

PATIENT POINT OF VIEW

Duke was a large breed dog who'd been on chemotherapy for five years. He was like a child to the older couple who shared his life and who'd poured their savings into his care. Toward the end of Duke's hospitalization, the man approached Michalski. "Our love for Duke might seem strange to you," he said, "but we can't understand how people can spend so much on a vacation and only have a suntan and some memories for it. We've had a real connection with Duke for many years and that's why we appreciate how you patiently answered our questions and showed us how to care for him and helped us through this time. We feel you understand how emotionally wrenching this is for us."

fast facts

What do you need?

- Creativity and resourcefulness for dealing with a variety of animal patients and their owners
- Ability to work closely with veterinarians
- Strong knowledge base in pharmacy and the willingness to compound prescriptions
- Ability to solve problems, prepare products, teach and consult with healthcare workers and pet owners

What's it take?

- A current, active license to practice pharmacy
- Bachelor of Science (BS) or Doctor of Pharmacy (PharmD) degree*
- Background in animal husbandry may be preferred
- Membership in the Society of Veterinary Hospital Pharmacists (SVHP) or American College of Veterinary Pharmacists (AVCP), and/or special training or certification by them may be preferred

Where will you practice?

- Specialized veterinary pharmacies
- Veterinary schools
- Animal clinics
- Animal hospitals
- Rescue centers
- Universities
- Compounding pharmacies
- Chain pharmacies

*Students graduating after Spring 2004 will be required to have a PharmD degree

the pharmacist in
management

the pharmacist in management

Pharmacists today have unparalleled opportunities in management as well as in patient care. But along with the diverse array of opportunities come responsibilities and accountabilities more complex and greater than any time in the past. On a broad palette, people with pharmacy degrees are being sought after by a host of industries — from insurance to computers;

from automation industries to government — that had not previously considered them. An increasing number of other channels for job recruitment are being directed at pharmacists as well. The result is a multitude of pharmacists who have elected to become specialists or who have moved up to the managerial level of pharmacy. Those individuals who choose to be specialists and managers generally need advanced postgraduate education in formal degree programs, and are actively seeking these degrees.

As in every field, pharmacy managers have to deal with and keep abreast of ever-changing issues, practice policies and new technologies. In pharmacy, these include the understanding of every new drug that comes to market. The number of these available new drugs has expanded exponentially, and the outcomes attendant on their use are unparalleled. People who might have died from an ailment in the past survive today because of these new therapeutic options. Another factor to be incorporated in the managing pharmacist's purview is an increasingly aged population in this country, which has dramatically driven up the demand for more and better health-care services. An increase in the number of patients needing medical services leads to a need for more people to serve them. On still another level, the expectations for positive therapeutic outcomes and financial consequences are on a higher plane now, so managers must be increasingly attentive to areas such as purchasing, distribution and assessment of outcomes. Managers in insurance, for example, will be chiefly concerned with policy issues, which are concentrated on getting the greatest benefit for the lowest cost. Whereas a single hospital clinic might focus on how to treat the patient best and most cost effectively, managers must concern themselves with the cost of the newest drugs and how best to get them to the patients who need them but who may not be able to afford them.

By Henri R. Manasse, Jr., PhD, ScD, RPh, Executive Vice President and Chief Executive Officer, American Society of Health System Pharmacists

Today's managers must rethink the labor issue. There is clearly a scarcity of pharmacists, a lack which makes it critical to keep those pharmacists currently on staff happy and engaged in their work environments. Due to the shortage, there is a growing need everywhere for supervisors to re-engineer their work forces, developing systems that allow and encourage the best qualified people to do the most important work, that provide strong support staff, and have technology-oriented people doing the more routine operations. Pharmacists cannot and should not work in isolation, and it's up to the administrative manager to set the path that blends them and the support staff into interdisciplinary-health teams.

Money remains a major concern and brings to the fore the problem of supplying a patient's need for infinite resources with a company's finite resources. The modern administrator is faced with having to make crucial decisions about what his or her employer can afford. There is no question that today's pharmacy managers have to do considerably more with less. Every organization within medicine, it seems, is working with a shortage of both money and staff. This is a situation that usually can be surmounted with some creativity and discipline.

Whether in the position of supervisor or general pharmacist, we must always remember that pharmacy is a people business. We deal with patients, physicians, nurses, administrators, public policy setters, regulators, and the like. For my part, the most complex and critical management issues have to do with my staff — struggling with letting some go, disciplining others and celebrating in the success of those with great talent. Sometimes, when I get to work in the morning, I think that after 30 years in this business — in academic, industry and association management — I have seen it all. Then my day starts and a plethora of unfamiliar and interesting issues arise which I am charged with overseeing. Despite the many challenges or perhaps because of them, I find pharmacy today as invigorating as the day I started in this field.

Henri R. Manasse, Jr., PhD has been Executive Vice President and Chief Executive Officer of the American Society of Health-System Pharmacists in Bethesda, Maryland since July 1997. Born in Amsterdam, The Netherlands, Manasse, who received a PhD in Pharmacy Administration from the University of Minnesota, had previously been Chairman of the Board of the University of Iowa Health System.

In a career that spans three decades, he has been Vice President for Health Sciences at The University of Iowa; Interim Vice Chancellor for Health Services at the University of Illinois at Chicago Health Sciences Center; and Senior Policy Fellow at the University of Maryland Center on Drugs and Public Policy in Baltimore. Dr. Manasse has also been Dean and Professor of Pharmacy Administration, Preventive Medicine and Environmental Health at the University of Illinois College of Pharmacy. He taught at the University of Minnesota College of Pharmacy in Minneapolis and was a research and production pharmacist at Xttrium Laboratories in Chicago. He chairs the board of the National Patient Safety Foundation and served on the Committee on Pharmacokinetics, Pharmacodynamics and Drug Interaction in the Elderly at the National Academy of Sciences Institute of Medicine. He is a medical and healthcare advisor for the U.S. Department of Veterans Affairs and has been President and Chairman of the Board of the American Association of Colleges of Pharmacy. He received an MA in educational psychology from Loyola University of Chicago in 1972 and a BS in Pharmacy in 1968 from the University of Illinois.

the pharmacist in management

professional, civic and
political leadership

By Bill K.
Brewster, CEO
and Chairman
of FH/GPC
Consultants
and Lobbyists

If you want to make a difference in the pharmacy industry, if you want to see change of any kind, you must be the one to effect it. Effecting change is something close to my heart. After all, I was a U.S. Congressman, representing Oklahoma's third district in the House for six years attempting to do just that. For a pharmacist, that means you have to step out from behind your desk, leave your store or practice site, and become involved beyond your day-to-day role as a pharmacist. What creates a good leader? Some key first steps include becoming active in your community, joining and being active in your professional associations, and keeping abreast of what is happening in your field and in the world. Incidentally, from a strictly professional standpoint, being active in your community and associations is extremely good for business.

Leadership is a little bit instinct and a little bit learning. If you have the instinct, you're halfway home. As far as that other half? Anyone can learn. First, I would encourage every one of you to take a speech class while you are still in college. You may wonder how this relates to pharmacy, but I cannot stress the importance of being comfortable talking to a group of people, whether it's the local Lions Club, or your state pharmacy association or potential business partners.

My first elected position was on a school board in Texas and my first speech was in front of two hundred people. It was a very simple speech, outlining my new ideas for handling school operations. But because I never had the benefit of a speech class, I was scared to death. On the day of the speech, every minute I wasn't filling prescriptions, I was in the back of my store scribbling on note cards and practicing bits and pieces. The night of the speech, I surprised myself. Not only did I get through it, I did pretty well. The lesson: We learn by doing but being well-prepared makes it a whole lot easier to put yourself out there.

Politics actually helped my professional life. Though friends warned me that running for the school board would hurt my pharmacy business, in fact, just the opposite occurred. Campaigning, I went out and met many people I had never met before in our fast-growing community. As a result, during this period, my pharmacy had one of its biggest growth spurts ever.

People skills are essential for a future leader. Get involved in college with any organization that gives you the opportunity to meet new people.

Consider joining the American Pharmaceutical Association (APhA) or American Society of Health System Pharmacists (ASHP) group in your pharmacy college. More than anything else, leadership means getting involved. College organizations offer you your first opportunity to do just that. It doesn't mean you have to be the president. It simply means you are actively engaged.

Once you launch your professional career, join your local pharmacy associations, including the APhA, ASHP, or the National Community Pharmacists

Association (NACP). All three send delegates to their state conventions from every state affiliate. Again, getting involved on state, local and national levels gives you a good perspective as well as opportunities to network. When I first graduated college, I worked for a chain of pharmacies in Dallas. I joined the Dallas county pharmacy association, started attending meetings and had the opportunity to interact with

independent pharmacists, hospital pharmacists, and chain pharmacists. This broad cross-section helped me to understand what was happening in my profession. When I later opened my own pharmacy in Tarrant County, Texas, I became active in the Tarrant County Pharmacy Association. That experience gave me the confidence to run for my first political office.

I've mentioned my first elected position on the Grapevine, Texas school board. After several years, I sold my pharmacy and moved to a ranch in Oklahoma where, in addition to ranching, I worked two to three days as a pharmacist. (One of the beauties of pharmacy is that you have these kinds of options.) When the state legislator from my district retired, I decided to run for his seat, and I won.

For the next eight years, I served in the Oklahoma state legislature. Because the state legislature is in session only four months out of the year, I was able to continue a part-time pharmacy practice during that entire period. In 1990, when the congressional representative from my district retired, I ran for Congress, and won again.

As a congressional representative, you do not live full-time in Washington, D.C. — rather you travel back and forth between your home and the Capital. Back home in Oklahoma, I continued to put in one or two days a month at a friend's retail pharmacy. It was good for me — it kept me fresh as far as pharmacy was concerned — and, likewise, it allowed my friend some time off.

Currently, I work as a lobbyist in Washington. I envision some day returning to pharmacy work in Texas or Oklahoma. That is another wonderful aspect of this profession: you can do it in a small community, in a large urban area, and if you are licensed, in any state of this beautiful country. You can practice half-time, part-time, or full-time or you can practice nights or days. You can even do it while you are a member in good standing of the United States Congress. You can take pharmacy with you wherever you go.

A final comment: You cannot be a good leader without getting someone to follow you. Just because you head out in a certain direction does not mean other people will accompany you on your journey. You must stay fresh. Get to know as many people as you can. Hear what they have to say. Listen. Speak up. And most of all — get involved.

Bill Brewster, a pharmacist and cattle rancher, started his career in public service when elected to his local school board in Grapevine, Texas in 1973. He spent eight years in the Oklahoma State Legislature where he served as chair of the Economic Development Committee as well as chair of the Southwest Energy Council. In 1990, he was elected to the U.S. Congress. Bill Brewster represented Oklahoma's 3rd District in the U.S. House of Representatives where he served on the Ways and Means Committee and the Transportation and Infrastructure Committee. While in Congress, Mr. Brewster chaired the Congressional Sportsmen's Caucus, the Oil and Gas Forum, and he was a co-founder of the Blue Dog Coalition (a group of pro-business Democrats). He chose to retire from public office in 1997 and is currently CEO and Chairman of FH/GPC Consultants and Lobbyists, a pharmacy lobbying organization, in Washington, DC.

challenges through time

In ancient times, when pharmacists practiced in a rudimentary form, they were responsible for making drugs, administering them, and maintaining the quality of the drugs dispensed. The origin of the word "pharmacy" from the Greek *pharmakon,* means remedy, and from the Egyptian term *ph-ar-maki* means bestower of security. Pharmacy and the practice of medicine were often combined, sometimes under the direction of priests. In AD 754, the first apothecary shop was established in Baghdad, marking the growing division of the professions of pharmacy and medicine with pharmacists moving into alchemy and ultimately chemistry. In 12th-century Europe, public pharmacies began to appear and in 1240, laws (later known as the Magna Carta of pharmacy) separated physicians from pharmacists whose elixirs, spirits, and powders were later described in the *Pharmacopeia of London* (1618) and the *Pharmacopeia of Paris* (1639).

By Elizabeth K. Keyes, RPh, Group Director Strategic Alliances and Industry Relations, American Pharmaceutical Association

After the American Revolution, European pharmacists began to emigrate to the United States. In 1821 the first college of pharmacy in the United States — the Philadelphia College of Pharmacy — was founded to assure training and supervision of pharmacists (The Pharmacopeia of the United States, was first published in 1820 and the National Formulary, published by the American Pharmaceutical Association, in 1888.)

The Industrial Revolution led to the creation of new drugs, standardized dosages of existing drugs and the introduction of mass marketed pharmaceuticals, all of which seemed to bring costs down. The result was more access to medicines for patients who earlier might not have been able to afford or obtain them.

Today's pharmacist plays an increasingly more important role in the American healthcare system. It is a role that offers exciting challenges and unlimited opportunity for branching out. In addition to patient care and counseling the pharmacist works within the ever growing business environment of today's pharmacy. Whether a community drug store, a chain, or within the walls of a great university hospital complex, the pharmacist is charged with a singular mission: He or she must ensure the right medication for each and every person is delivered in the appropriate manner. Understanding the mechanisms of action and clinical characteristics of a drug is critical to understanding the very nature of drug interactions, side effects and other complex issues. We owe this to our patients.

Technology poses new challenges to the pharmacist as well. Cutting edge technology advances properly integrated into the workplace will help the profession, but today pharmacists still need assistance, in the form of technicians and other ancillary personnel to free them up to see patients. This is especially difficult as pharmacists meet with heavier work loads: more and more prescriptions are being dispensed, hospital stays are shorter, and America's population base is aging.

The important responsibility of educator has now been factored into the pharmacist's role. The Internet, for all its good points, often dispenses invalid information when it comes to healthcare. Many of the disease related "research articles" which people seek and find on the web are not scientific. Most are not even signed. Another source of consumer information is prescription drug advertising. While this empowers patients by getting them to talk with their health care providers and helps solve problems of under-diagnosis and treatment, it can lead some patients to have questions about taking medications they may not need.

Lastly a morass of regulatory issues faces the industry. In some states, pharmacists have more authority and practice flexibility than they do in other states. For example, 31 states have granted pharmacists the authority to immunize patients to safeguard them against vaccine-preventable illness. Our association is working to make these regulations more uniform and help pharmacists expand their patient care activities.

This new age poses ethical quandaries, of course. But the basic challenge remains — making sure we get the right drug to the right patient at the right time. I often work with interns, externs and summer residents, and the main message I give them is that it's important to network in order to have a real impact on their future. Becoming involved in your profession is the best window to what is out there. Always look to the next step in your career; stay open to traditional and non-traditional opportunities. Networking and involvement in professional organizations will not only enable you to find out about these opportunities, but will give you a head start in securing them. Look at these options as stepping stones, opportunities to grow and learn.

Today is unquestionably the golden age of pharmacy. There are enormous numbers of opportunities for pharmacists as they increasingly move to patient care and expanding realms of responsibility within their communities and managed care. Ironically, roles in the healthcare arena are merging again as in historical times; pharmacists now share many direct patient-service responsibilities with other members of the healthcare team. This transitioning is making pharmacists increasingly relevant to today's brave new healthcare world.

Elizabeth K. Keyes has been with the American Pharmaceutical Association in Washington DC since 1993. She has been responsible for clinical program design, professional continuing education administration, and development of marketing and communication strategies for pharmaceutical industry partners. She currently directs the development, management and execution of APhA's certificate education programs and coordinates marketing and sales of education programs to key pharmaceutical industry manufacturers and chain pharmacies. Before joining the association in 1993, Ms. Keyes worked as a pharmacist for the CVS chain in Alexandria, Virginia and before that as a Pharmacy Intern at Rite Aid Pharmacy in Morgantown, West Virginia. She received a Bachelor of Science in General Science — Biology from Wheeling Jesuit University, Wheeling, WV in 1989 and a Bachelor of Science in Pharmacy from West Virginia University, Morgantown, WV in 1991.

organizations
and resources

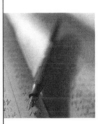

organizations and resources

A

**Academy of Managed Care
Pharmacy (AMCP)**
100 North Pitt Street, Suite 400
Alexandria, VA 22314
(800) 827-2627

**American Association of Colleges of
Pharmacy (AACP)**
1426 Prince Street
Alexandria, VA 22314
(703) 739-2330

**American Association of
Pharmaceutical Scientists (AAPS)**
1650 King Street, Suite 200
Alexandria, VA 22314-2747
(703) 548-3000

**American Association of Pharmacy
Technicians, Inc. (AAPT)**
P.O. Box 1447
Greensboro, NC 27402
(336) 275-1700

American Chemical Society (ACS)
1155 16th Street N.W., Suite 400
Washington, DC 20036
(202) 872-4600

**American College
of Apothecaries (ACA)**
P.O. Box 341266
Memphis, TN 38184
(901) 383-8119

**American College of Clinical
Pharmacy (ACCP)**
3101 Broadway, Suite 380
Kansas City, MO 64111
(816) 531-2177

**American Council on
Pharmaceutical Education (ACPE)**
311 West Superior Street, Suite 512
Chicago, IL 60610
(312) 664-3575

**American Foundation for
Pharmaceutical Education (AFPE)**
1 Church Street, Suite 202
Rockville, MD 20850
(301) 738-2160

**American Pharmaceutical
Association (APhA)**
2215 Constitution Avenue N.W.
Washington, DC 20037
(202) 628-4410

**American Public Health
Association (APHA)**
1015 15th Street N.W., Suite 300
Washington, DC 20005
(202) 789-5600

**American Society for Automation
in Pharmacy (ASAP)**
492 Norristown Road, Suite 160
Blue Bell, PA 19422-2359
(610) 825-7783

American Society of Consultant Pharmacists (ASCP)
1321 Duke Street
Alexandria, VA 22314-3563
(703) 739-1300

American Society of Health-System Pharmacists (ASHP)
7272 Wisconsin Avenue
Bethesda, MD 20814
(301) 657-3000

American Society for Parenteral & Enteral Nutrition (ASPEN)
8630 Fenton Street, Suite 412
Silver Spring, MD 20910-3805
(301) 587-6315

American Society for Pharmacy Law (ASPL)
P.O. Box 1726
Valley Center, CA 92082
(760) 742-1470

B

Board of Pharmaceutical Specialties (BPS)
2215 Constitution Avenue N.W.
Washington, DC 20037-2985
(202) 429-7591

C

Chain Drug Marketing Association, Inc. (CDMA)
43157 West Nine Mile Road
P.O. Box 995
Novi, MI 48376-0995
(248) 449-9300

Council on Family Health
225 Park Avenue South, 17th Floor
New York, NY 10003
(212) 598-3617

D

Drug, Chemical and Allied Trades Association (DCAT)
2 Roosevelt Avenue, Suite 301
Syosset, NY 11791
(516) 496-3317

F

Food and Drug Law Institute (FDLI)
1000 Vermont Avenue N.W.,
Suite 200
Washington, DC 20005
(202) 371-1420

Food Industry Association Executives (FIAE)
P.O. Box 2510
Flemington, NJ 08822
(908) 782-7833

G

Grocery Manufacturers of America, Inc. (GMA)
1010 Wisconsin Avenue N.W.,
Suite 900
Washington, DC 20007
(202) 337-9400

H

Health Industry Manufacturers Association (HIMA)
1200 G Street N.W., Suite 400
Washington, DC 20005
(202) 783-8700

I

The International Academy of Compounding Pharmacists (IACP)
P.O. Box 1365
Sugar Land, TX 77487
(281) 933-8400
(800) 927-4227

International Pharmaceutical Federation (FIP)
Andries Bickerweg 5
2517 JP The Hague
The Netherlands
(31) (70) 302-1970

International Society for Pharmacoeconomic and Outcomes Research (ISPOR)
20 Nassau Street, Suite 307
Princeton, NJ 08542
(609) 252-1305

Institute for the Advancement of Community Pharmacy
9687 South Run Oaks Drive
Fairfax Station, VA 22039
(703) 690-2559

N

National Association of Boards of Pharmacy (NABP)
700 Busse Highway
Park Ridge, IL 60068
(847) 698-6227

National Association of Chain Drug Stores (NACDS)
413 North Lee Street
P.O. Box 1417-D49
Alexandria, VA 22313-1480
(703) 549-3001

National Association of Pharmaceutical Manufacturers (NAPM)
320 Old Country Road, Suite 205
Garden City, NY 11530-1743
(516) 741-3699

National Community Pharmacists
Association (NCPA)
205 Daingerfield Road
Alexandria, VA 22314
(703) 683-8200

National Conference of
Pharmaceutical Organizations
(NCPO)
c/o NDMA
1150 Connecticut Avenue N.W.
Washington, DC 20036-4193
(202) 429-9260

National Council for Prescription
Drug Programs (NCPDP)
4201 North 24th Street, Suite 365
Phoenix, AZ 85016-6266
(602) 957-9105

National Council on the Aging
(NCOA)
409 Third Street S.W., Suite 200
Washington, DC 20024
(202) 479-1200

National Council of State Pharmacy
Association Executives (NCSPAE)
c/o Ohio Pharmacists Association
6037 Frantz Road, Suite 106
Dublin, OH 43017
(614) 798-0037

National Council on Patient
Information and Education (NCPIE)
4915 Saint Elmo Avenue, Suite 505
Bethesda, MD 20814-6053
(301) 656-8565

National Grocers Association
(NGA)
1825 Samuel Morse Drive
Reston, VA 20190-5317
(703) 437-5300

National Institute for Pharmacist
Care Outcomes (NIPCO)
205 Daingerfield Road
Alexandria, VA 22314
(703) 683-8200

National Pharmaceutical
Association (NPhA)
The Courtyards Office Complex
107 Kilmayne Drive, Suite C
Cary, NC 27511
(800) 944-6742

National Pharmaceutical
Council, Inc. (NPC)
1894 Preston White Drive
Reston, VA 20191-5433
(703) 620-6390
Fax: (703) 476-0904
www.npcnow.org

National Wholesale Druggists'
Association (NWDA)
1821 Michael Faraday Drive,
Suite 400
Reston, VA 20190-5348
(703) 787-0000

Nonprescription Drug
Manufacturers Association (NDMA)
1150 Connecticut Avenue N.W.
Washington, DC 20036-4193
(202) 429-9260

P

Parenteral Drug Association (PDA)
7500 Old Georgetown Road,
Suite 620
Bethesda, MD 20814-6133
(301) 986-0293

The Pediatric Pharmacy Advocacy
Group, Inc.
9866 West Victoria Drive
Littleton, CO 80128
(720) 981-7356

Pharmaceutical Care Management
Association (PCMA)
2300 Ninth Street South, Suite 210
Arlington, VA 22204-2320
(703) 920-8480

Pharmaceutical Research and
Manufacturers of America
(PhRMA)
1100 15th Street N.W., Suite 900
Washington, DC 20005
(202) 835-3400

Professional Compounding
Centers of America
9901 South Wilcrest
Houston, TX 77099
(800) 331-2498

U

United States Pharmacopeia (USP)
12601 Twinbrook Parkway
Rockville, MD 20852-1790
(301) 881-0666 x8250

W

Western Association of
Food Chains (WAFC)
825 Colorado Boulevard, Suite 203
Los Angeles, CA 90041-1714
(323) 254-7279